"There is little disagreement that the best golf writer of all time was an Englishman named Bernard Darwin. Beyond this, there is a large body of readers, made up not only of golf addicts but of addicts of other sports, who believe that Bernard Darwin may well be the finest talent who has ever written about sports, not excluding such towering figures as William Hazlitt, Leo Tolstoy, William Faulkner, Siegfried Sassoon, and Ernest Hemingway . . ."

Herbert Warren Wind

FLAGSTICK BOOKS

Original Edition of

The Happy Golfer

A Collection of Articles from
The American Golfer Magazine
1922–1936

By
Bernard Darwin

Introduction by Frank Pennink

Edited by Robert S. Macdonald
Assisted by Ian R. Macdonald

"To know that you have done it is the best thing; to know that you ought to do it is something; to know that you ought to have done it—there is mighty little help in that."

"For, after all, we do play golf for fun."

Bernard Darwin

To

L.A.M., I.R.M., C.S.M.

Editor's Note

Bernard Darwin is a great writer writing about the game he loves more than anything else in life, and all he sees are the ordinary things in golf. To our surprise these ordinary things are precisely the ones we do not see. They are right in front of our noses, and we go right by them. Not only do we miss them but, on those occasions when we do recognize them, we are reluctant to point them out for fear of making ourselves look petty or foolish. This, of course, is what great writers do for us. They ask the questions we are embarrassed to ask. They restore to us the reality of a world we do not see or do not wish to admit we see.

The Introduction is by Frank Pennink, who was born in Delft, Netherlands in 1913. He attended Oxford and played for the University Golf Team in 1933, 1934, and 1935. He won the English Amateur championship in 1937 and 1938. He was one of the victorious Walker Cup Team of 1938. He was golf correspondent of the *Sunday Express* and *Daily Mail*, served on many committees of The Royal and Ancient Golf Club, was president of the English Golf Union in 1967, and became a distinguished and successful golf-course architect with the firm of Cotton, Pennink, Lawrie and Partners. He designed the West Course at Saunton, the scene of Darwin's last essay in "The Happy Golfer," A Town on the Sand. He was Darwin's close friend for thirty years. He wrote this article, which we use for our Introduction, for a British publication in 1962, not long after Darwin's death.

Robert S. Macdonald

INTRODUCTION

By Frank Pennink

"I saw the first two holes—and then it was time for tea."

No doubt the sports editor of the London *Times* blanched—to say the least—when he received this cryptic message from his correspondent on the scene of the 1934 British Open. He might have even suspected that the last word was misspelled, further adding to the confusion.

Yet, knowing the man on the other end of the wire, the editor knew the story would eventually be colorfully and knowingly reported.

Bernard Darwin, he of rigid convictions, was the man who placed that message. Always willing to put a too-wise professional in his rightful place or cool off an impatient editor—Darwin was Great Britain's golf-writing bellwether for more than 50 years prior to his death at 85 last October.

Bernardo—as he was known by his friends—was no arrogant man, but in his own quaint and diverting ways was wont to indicate that he knew his position as the game's chief scribe. How else could you describe a man who not only faithfully reported important links events for such an extensive period, but at the same time gained a reputation as an essayist of the highest literary quality?

Perhaps his indominitable spirit was a legacy from his grandfather, Sir Charles Darwin of "Origin of Species" fame. Whatever its source, British golf literature gained immeasurably.

Born Sept. 7, 1876, in Kent, Darwin studied law at Cambridge but practiced this profession for only a few years. A skilled golfer himself, Darwin decided at an early date that journalism was his cup of tea.

When I first met Bernardo I was an Oxford freshman of 1931. Like everyone else familiar with his repute, I held him in the deepest awe and with fearful respect. He knew the Rules of Golf backwards and forwards and, though in his mid-fifties, was still a fine player himself. Years of writing for the *Times* were behind him. To be introduced to Darwin was, to an undergraduate, akin to being received at court, although that was the last impression he wished to create.

Already I had heard many of the celebrated anecdotes about him. I knew how chance had given him the right to wear that famous necktie with the red eagles and lions on a navy blue background—that of the Walker Cup team.

In the summer of 1922 Bernardo sailed with the British Walker Cup team as his newspaper's correspondent. When the captain of the British team, Robert Harris, fell ill on the eve of the matches, Darwin took his place as player and counsellor. Bernardo's move was not presumptive from the playing standpoint, for the year before he had reached the semi-finals of the British Amateur for the second time.

Darwin and Cyril Tolley suffered a heavy defeat at the hands of the renowned U.S. team of Jesse Guilford and Francis Ouimet, but the writer made amends by beating W. C. Fownes in the singles.

Perhaps his greatest feat of those few days, however, was the writing of two full columns on the match for his newspaper. Those of us who have attempted to both play and write know the trying difficulties imposed by such a dual role.

Some years later—in 1934—I had a chance to personally ascribe to his deftness at this writing-playing trick.

We were members of the Oxford and Cambridge Golfing Society team on its tour of Scotland. I was a third-year undergraduate, and Bernardo was captain of the team. We were chosen to form a partners team against the Luffness New Golf Club. He wrote thus in the *Times*:

"One of the most singular matches was the fourth. Darwin and Pennink began by going gloriously and completely mad against Rose and Drybrough. They holed the first seven holes in 24 shots and stood six-up. Then occurred something analogous to the great landslide between More and Jamieson in the University Match.

"Rose and Drybrough buckled up and playing four holes very well won them all. That was down to two, and it would be flattery to pretend that their opponents did not feel uncomfortable. However, they rallied sufficiently to hang onto those two precious holes, all that was left of their once princely fortune, and scrambled home by two and one humbly and gratefully."

I write, from memory crystal clear of that match, that awe froze me into a minimum of errors, and it was one of those days when the hole seemed bucket-sized to us both. While we were losing our long lead, Bernardo went back on his heels, strayed behind and began to mutter to himself. As the match became closer his utterings became louder and fiercer until they were quite audible to the three competitors walking ahead of him.

His monologue ran something like this:

"Those conceited Oxford brats (meaning me)! They think they know all about the game, but as soon as they are under pressure they go to pieces." Then oaths and imprecations followed. My Oxford blood chilled.

When I came to play a delicate chip over a bunker, and fluffed the ball into the sand, I felt that the end of the world had come. I wouldn't have been surprised if Bernardo had come at me with an unpraised putter. Instead, there was deathly silence. When that nightmare match was over I breathed relief.

As he always was in the clubhouse after a match, Darwin seemed oblivious to his eccentricities on the links. He was his usual charming, courteous self, even going so far as to mention that he was particularly pleased to have won because he had maintained, at ten out of ten, his unbeaten record at Luffness.

Darwin's deadly serious love for Cambridge and British golf never let up. In his later years he became disenchanted with the professional side of golf and devoted his *Times* columns almost exclusively to the amateurs. His writing was always truthful, perhaps especially so when he penned his own deeds.

One such chance came in 1933, when he paired with the immaculate Joyce Wethered in the Worplesdon Mixed Foursomes. Although he was past his best, Bernardo was still a steady senior golfer in those days.

Their matches were at once a compliment and a trial to the wonderful Miss Wethered, surely the finest woman golfer of all time with her elegant and faultless style. Darwin played a good game but suffered torture on the greens. His awful putting had driven him to the extremes of putting with his mashie. Yet they won the tournament, and his writings of their victory, wherein the reader could feel the despair and humble rejoicing of Miss Wethered, are among the most gripping and yet amusing in the annals of golfing literature.

Since Hitler's war, Bernardo's golf amounted to little more than a few holes on his own, and finally to a small number of iron shots, taken unnoticed, up and down a fairway. Rheumatics and arthritis harshly restricted his movements.

In this last decade of his career, Darwin could not keep pace with a match. He would often overcome this disability by taking up a single vantage point and depend on friends to bring him news of the matches.

Inevitably dressed in knickerbockers, Darwin was still able to turn out interesting stories. Most of his literature is to be found in the pages of *Country Life* and *Golf Monthly* during this period, as in 1955 he had finally retired from the *Times* staff.

Future British Opens and Amateurs will not seem the

same without this gruff but kindly old man, out some-where on the course, storing up notes for his imperish-able prose. Bernardo was reluctant to recognize his dis-ability, but he would accept offers to be driven over the course. Many a new track was blazed to enable him to see as much as possible.

Darwin went down fighting, and with many honors. In 1937 he had been rewarded with the decoration of Commander of the British Empire. All felt his knight-hood was fully merited.

When he retired from the *Times*, friends gave him a dinner. The paper has an inviolable rule that disallows members of its staff to receive a notice in its columns upon retirement. No exception was made this time, al-though when one of the speakers made reference to this matter a wry smile crept across the face of Lord Astor, proprietor of the paper. The shot went home, all right.

It was not until six more years had passed, years of inconvenience and pain and indeed many bed-ridden months, that Bernardo received notice in the *Times*—in the obituary column.

One cannot say that Bernard Darwin raised the level of golf reporting for he was, in fact, the first golf writer— truly the "originator of the species."

Table of Contents

1936

1922

Three Great American Courses

In 1922, Grantland Rice asked Bernard Darwin to contribute to The American Golfer *magazine on a regular basis. This, his first article, appeared in the issue of September 9, 1922.*

The Editor has asked me to compare the Lido,* Pine Valley and the National Golf Links in Southampton, New York. Comparisons are dangerous things, especially when made by a guest who has innumerable kindnesses to be grateful for. I would rather say, therefore, that I will try to analyze some of the characteristics of these three great American courses.

The National was already an old friend, for I had played several days on it in 1913. The other two were new to me. If I were to sum up in a few words my personal impressions of the three I should say that Lido was the finest course in the world, Pine Valley the hardest course in the world and that I would rather play on the National than either of them.

Taking Lido first, the fact that the course is there at all is a standing miracle, the wonder of which will never fade. As one drives along that exceedingly bumpy road to Long Beach one sees the ground work of the course—a flat, green, slimy swamp—nothing more nor less. And yet there has been laid on the top of that foundation the sandiest of sea-side courses. Doubtless the laying of it was a wonderful feat of engineering, but still more wonderful in my eyes is the feat of imagination. Mr. C. B. Macdonald is more than an inspired architect. He must be a poet and a visionary as well to have dreamed such a dream.

The fact that Lido is right on the sea, that one could throw a pebble with one's left hand into the Atlantic from the Club

---

The Lido, designed by Charles B. Macdonald in 1917 on the south shore of Long Island, was considered to be one of America's very greatest courses. It no longer exists.

house windows will always prejudice British golfers in its favor. We have been brought up to believe that sea-side golf is
the real thing, that a sea-side wind provides the supreme test
and nothing will ever get that out of our heads. The bent grass
heeling over under the breeze is for us eminently friendly and
home like.

Yet making due allowance for this prejudice what fine holes
there are at Lido! How majestic and tremendous! How full of
variety and interest. Really I have only one criticism and I
will get it over at once—I do think that the rough is in a good
many places too thick. Not only is it tiresome to have to hunt
for a ball but it is a little monotonous to play always niblick
shots when you find it.

In England, where we are, I suppose, a softer run of golfers,
we have generally a kind of purgatory for the moderately sin-
ful player while the genuinely infernal regions are reserved for
the outrageous hook or slice. Out of the purgatory a player
who has skill and some fortune may be able to play a forcing
mashie (5 iron) and so lose something indeed but not a whole
stroke. In Lido's rough an error of but a few feet, nay inches
generally mean digging the ball out with the niblick (8 iron).
This is, I think, too severe for pleasure and perhaps for justice
as well.

That is all I have to say in criticism. The bunkering is as
fair as it is fine. There is never a dull shot to play as long as you
are on the fairway, not a hole where the extra good and bold
shot will not reap its proper reward. If I had to pick out any
particular holes I think they would be the fourth, sixth, seventh and eighteenth. The fourth is certainly the most majestic two-shot hole I have ever seen. Played as we played it in a
stiff cross wind it is truly awe-inspiring. Nobody but the really
fine wooden club player could hope to get up, but humble folk
have a way 'round. For them, the getting of a five will be full
of thrills. The hole is as interesting as it is impressive.

In the eighteenth I have a particular interest for a personal
reason. Just before the First World War, Mr. Macdonald offered me on behalf of *Country Life* magazine in England three

prizes to be awarded for the best designs for a two-shot hole. Mr. Horace Hutchinson, Mr. Herbert Fowler and I were the judges and a great many clever designs were sent in. We all agreed without hesitation on the best of all. When we opened the sealed envelope containing the designer's name we found that it was Dr. Mackenzie, now a partner of Mr. H. S. Colt. The hole that he made is now reproduced as the eighteenth at Lido and a great hole it is, with the big carry from the tee, three different tongues of grass to aim for, according to the wind and the player's driving power, and then for the long hitter a really glorious slash home onto a beautiful green. I was more than ever sure, when I saw it, that we were right in our award of the prize.

If the Lido course reminded us in one way of home so did Pine Valley in another. In Surrey at a range of twenty to thirty miles of London, we have a number of courses in which the two chief ingredients are sand and pine trees. Therefore the green glades of turf winding here and there amongst the firs are distinctly familiar to us though no one of our courses of this type is conceived on so big a scale as is Pine Valley. Here, too, there is more than architecture.

The late Mr. Crump must have had more than a touch of prophetic imagination as well. His was, I believe, the original conception and his design was modified by the advice of Mr. Colt and his partner, Mr. Alison. The result is truly remarkable, but in order thoroughly to appreciate it we must know what was in Mr. Crump's mind when he first thought of the course. This was, as we were told on our visit, that somewhere there ought to be one course where, as far as is humanly possible, the best man on the day should win because every bad or indifferent shot should meet with its reward. That is a high but a very severe ideal. It relegates mere pleasure in playing to a minor position and personally I think there are just one or two holes at Pine Valley which are too hard to be pleasant.

The tee shots are difficult but they are very interesting and not unfairly difficult. The rough is cruel indeed, and you may find yourself almost unplayable in the woodlands, but there is adequate room and the fault is yours. What we Britons were disposed to criticize was the almost fantastic severity of the traps guarding some of the greens. They are so close to the green, so omnipresent that it is dreadfully easy to get out of one into another and then back again to the end of the chapter. This almost amounts to eternal punishment and eternal punishment had better be left for the day of judgment.

The hole I have particularly in mind is the eighth where the green is very, very small and rather fast and sloping into the bargain. There really seems here no limit to the player's liabilities and there is a touch of trickiness and freakishness which is unworthy of so magnificent a course. In one or two other instances the undulations in the greens are too severe, but the eighth is the one real sinner. I admit that I took something more than an eight on it myself, but I hope that this has not warped my judgment.

Having got that off my chest I could write pages of admiration of many of its holes—the second, for instance, with its green perched so defiantly above a big sandy bluff; the eighteenth a really superb finish with a long second to be hit right home over a water jump and a big bunker; the thirteenth and sixth, two beautiful "dog leg" holes, both scrupulously fair.

Again what a memorable short hole is the fifth—one full spoon shot over a tremendous chasm stretching from tee to green, a wilderness of fir trees on the right, big bunkers on the left. To land the ball on that green—and there is no reason in the world why you should not do it if you are not frightened—provides a moment worth living for.

My final belief, right or wrong, is that the pleasure of playing Pine Valley would be greater if a few more concessions were made to human weakness. A game is not a competitive examination.

I have left myself very little space to write of the National which I love. Nine years ago the fairway was rather rough and the rough was the devil itself. Today the fairways are perfect, the rough is less fierce but quite fierce enough and the course has become rather shorter than of old because the ball flies still further. All these three things make in this instance for greater happiness. Compared with the other two courses I have described, the National is not very severe and yet every stroke has to be played rightly. The punishment is not so uniform and, as it seems to me, more discriminating. At the National, if you make a bad shot, you will not get off scot free but your punishment will take various shapes. It may be a niblick shot played merely to get out and a whole stroke gone; it may be a lie which will yield to a forcing iron shot; it may be not a bad lie at all but in such a position that the shot up to the green is intensely difficult. There may always be joy for the sinner who repents if he does so in a practical manner. In fact there is scope for all varieties of recovering shots and that surely adds intensely to the pleasure and interest of golf.

The National must always be interesting to British golfers because of the holes there which are founded on famous holes at home. There is the second which is the Sahara at Sandwich; the third is the Alps at Prestwick; the fourth is the Redan at North Berwick; the seventh and thirteenth are respectively the two most criticized and admired holes at St. Andrews, namely the seventeenth and eleventh. All these are very good but they are good in their own way rather than in that of their originals, because every course has its atmosphere which cannot be transplanted; and personally I think that the very best holes at the National are those which owe nothing to any model but spring entirely from the wonderful architectural genius of their "only begetter."

The Golfer and His Clothes

A week or two ago I went down to stay in the county with Mr. Tolley and Mr. Wethered and some other golfing friends for the opening of a new course. It was to be opened with a flourish of trumpets with a match between Mr. Tolley and Mr. Wethered. Both showed signs of an American golfing education by arriving at the first tee clad not in coats but in wooly waistcoats. At the fourth hole however Mr. Tolley appeared dressed entirely à l'Americain for he stripped off his waistcoat and flouted the autumn sunshine in a white cotton shirt. It was the first occasion as far as I know in which a British golfer in this country has played a serious match in shirt sleeves.

No doubt Mr. Tolley will do it again and if so his example may set a fashion in that admirable quality, common sense. If you feel too hot it makes sense to take your coat off. And yet we Britons are not quite so foolish as we must appear to you in playing with our coats on. We are not entirely slaves to tradition and prejudice. The superstition against walking under a ladder presumably had its origin in some unfortunate gentleman who did so and had a pot of paint dropped on his head. Similarly our superstition—if you like to call it so—on the coat question comes partly from the fact that the man, who is used to playing in a coat and suddenly takes it off, plays as a rule very badly.

Since our climate is not often hot enough to make a coat a burden, it seems hardly worth our while, especially as we are a conservative race, to experiment. Those who habitually play coatless do not realize what a curious situation it is. When we came to America this last summer, we practiced the art and our first efforts were truly singular. I shall not forget Mr. Robert Harris' first effort—I think at Piping Rock on a stifling hot day. The club went swishing beautifully up to the top of the

7

swing; then he gave a yell of dismay and the ball hurtled far into the rough. It is the coming down that is so disconcerting. It is like coming down a roller-coaster at Coney Island. You feel that the club is running away with you and that you are falling to pieces.

It is only a matter of practice to overcome this alarming feeling but no American can appreciate how alarming it is at first, any more than a Briton can appreciate the difficulties of playing in a coat. I met this summer American golfers who told me that they had never tried to swing in a coat and did not know what in the world would happen if they did. This appeared to me ridiculous, but they were no more ridiculous than I was—we were both slaves of habit.

How much this clothing question is a matter of habit I realize when I remember my golf at school at Eton. Our regular costume consisted amongst other things, of a black tail coat, a top hat, a stiff white shirt. The hat and the tail coat could be removed and a cap and a tweed coat substituted but time was limited, and there was no time for more changing. So the white shirt remained with its front of cast iron. Moreover I had not got any shoes with nails. I used to play in button boots with smooth soles on the slimiest and muddiest of courses. If any one had put it into my mind that I could not possibly have played in such an outfit, I doubt I could have. Ignorance being bliss, I thought nothing about it and played tolerably well.

Meanwhile I think that the woolly waistcoat is going to be a serious rival to the coat in this country. Perhaps the time will come when Oxford and Cambridge golfers will play against one another attired in dark and light blue waistcoats respectively.

One thing there is to be said against them. They have lamentably few and inadequate pockets. Where is the pipe to go and the pouch and the matches and the spare ball, in case you drive out of bounds, and the bit of pitch to rub on your grips—which incidentally always get too hot and sticky and adheres to your pipe and ruins your pouch—where are they all to go? In the caddie's pocket perhaps, but I distrust the caddies' pockets. I suspect that there are other sticky things such as a half sucked bit of toffee there. Some people burden their caddie with a satchel such as a child takes to school but this complicates life. No, I must say I should miss the pockets of my old coat.

And then again is there not something eminently lovable and engaging in an old golfing coat? An old waistcoat merely looks dirty but an old coat full of stains and crumples seems to me picturesque. It becomes in time extraordinarily characteristic of its owner. One comes to know every fold of the coats of the illustrious. I could swear to Mr. Hilton's green stockinet jacket anywhere, as I could have once to Mr. Johnny Low's black-white check. Braid has had generations of grey coats with a sort of pleat down the back. I should as soon expect to see the great man pirouetting in knickerbockers as to see him in any other kind of coat.

If these distinguished garments were to be shed for mere waistcoats or jerseys I should feel a sentimental regret, but I confess to feeling very little over the red coat which has almost entirely vanished. The great men did not—at least when I can remember them—wear red coats. It was the old and wrinkled shooting jacket that ever marked the golfer. The man who had a red coat with facings of some beautiful color and shiny gold buttons complete was generally the earnest student who had just done his first round under a hundred.

To be sure I was fond and proud of one red coat. It was my own. It had a light blue color and on the pocket were worked in gold and scarlet and ermine the arms of the University of Cambridge. Together with a light blue cap bearing silver crossed clubs—which no one in my time had the temerity to wear out of doors—it signified that one had played against Oxford. Alas! not only has my own particular coat long since fallen a victim to the corrupting moth but a modern Cambridge undergraduate would as soon be seen playing golf in his cap and gown as in a shirt!

In one or two places the red coat still lingers. There is a pretty little course at Esher, dotted with bracken and gorse, which I often pass either by rail or road. Here the golfers are compelled to clothe themselves in scarlet as a danger signal. Again at the royal Wimbledon Club the custom still survives and there is something pleasantly archaic as well as actually pretty in those splashes of red upon the green. At Blackheath too, the original home of golf in England, an occasional red-coated old gentleman may still be seen steering his difficult way between public roads and omnibuses and small boys playing football. I fear that golf on this historic heath is now almost as moribund as that historic garment. "How for all things there is a time and a season." I suppose I must go out and buy a woolly waistcoat. I shall have to come to it sooner or later.

Green Christmases

I am writing this article towards the end of November. By the time it reaches New York December will have come in and you will be thinking of Christmas. I am already thinking about my Christmas golf and reflecting in an unchristian and gloating spirit, that perchance some of my American friends will be snowed up or frozen out, while I am away to Wales—to the sea, for the jolliest week's golf of the year. Indeed this is a selfish article which I write entirely for my own pleasure.

To be quite accurate, this golfing party of mine will begin just after Christmas. The same party has met in the house of the same kind host since some time at the end of the last century. One member of the party celebrated a year or two ago his twenty-first consecutive annual visit, and I might have equalled his record but for the war years. I remember we had been promised Madeira of Waterloo year to drink in 1915 and I had to put off my share till 1919. In a gathering so old established there must be some regrets. There have come one or two gaps in our numbers and the collective golf of the party, which was not very good even in its comparatively youthful prime, is not so good as it used to be. Neither is it so energetic.

Time was when we dashed down to the course after an early breakfast, bearing with us bottles of a soothing and agreeable shape to supplement our lunch, played our two singles for certain and then, when some felt a passing weakness towards home and tea, we were marshalled by our inexorable host, paired off and sent out again to play a nine hole foursome. Today alas! Some of the party of which I am the baby, play but one round, climb the hill again for lunch and stay there. Moreover the last rubber at night used never to end till we had heard the chimes of the old church clock at midnight. Now there is a disposition to sneak away, with many heartfelt yawns, soon after eleven.

Nos et senescimus annis. It cannot be helped, but if we play less we enjoy ourselves quite as much as we can. There is the

11

same thrill in the packing of clubs and the start of the journey. The same Christmas like exuberance as we who start from London pick up some of our numbers at Birmingham and then at Shrewsbury and so, in an infinitely leisurely and dawdling train, chug over the Welsh border. Sometimes we start in frost and fog or even snow and then what delight to see it disappear to find warmth and a soft gray sky and a gentle wind as we near our haven.

When we are nearly home there is a certain hill up which the train pants more laboriously than ever. Once over the crest we feel that we can almost snuff the salt in the air, and the train rattles joyously down to the coast. It has happened to us once to travel through a white snow-clad land all the way from London till we reached that hill-top and then on the other side to find a green paradise awaiting us.

That was truly a moment when life was worth living; a better moment perhaps, since anticipation is always better than reality, than any to be enjoyed afterwards. And yet the golf is wonderfully pleasant. Ours is a fine piece of natural golfing ground, even though the best has never quite been made of it, undulating and rippling in a hundred grassy hummocks and hollows with noble sandhills, crowned with spiky bents, and little dell-like crater greens that nestle among the hills. There perchance the ball which is hit something too strongly will run round and lie by the hole side at last, to give us a three where a five should have been our portion—a birdie undeserved but none the less sweet for that.

And then how green it all looks, with a kind of dewy, winter freshness. All signs of parching summer are gone, there are no hard dusty yellow patches. The turf is soft and yielding, the ball sits up asking to be hit and hit it we must, for there is now little run in the ground and a two-shot hole is a two-shot hole.

Then too we have the course very nearly to ourselves. There are no competitions to agitate our nerves. We play only our own lazily friendly matches. We can start when we like: we can cut in where we please. Gone are the battalions of holiday makers who in the summer time wage a fierce warfare—the outgoing against the incoming—in the narrow neck where the fourth and the fourteenth holes meet. We have played there so long that we feel that we have a prescriptive, immemorial right to it and now the place really does belong to us. How we do hate those summer intruders. What do they know of our paradise who have come for just one year or two?

There in the village street walks a portly and dignified figure in black. To the summer folk he appears merely a Minister but we remember him as a little sandy haired caddy boy, called "Ginger" who used to carry Cornelius Nepos in his pocket and study the classics between his master's shots. We can remember when there was no clubhouse, when no ball had ever been struck over that hill, now shored up with black sleepers, which today is famous, when there were only flower pots instead of tins in the holes.

What do those upstarts know of those historic times? It is our links, and we made it.

In the Rough

There are no two expressions more frequently in the mouths of golfers than "fairway" and "rough" and there always seems something surprising about the fact that neither of them is to be found in the rules of golf. That most dreadful enemy, the rough, which probably slays its tens of thousands, has no legal existence. In law it is exactly on a footing with the smoothest and most beautiful piece of turf in the very middle of the course.

This seems today surprising and yet, without sounding too terribly old, I can remember the time when "the rough" was neither a regular expression nor a regular thing. In the 1880s and early 1890s it was quite the exception to find clear cut areas of rough grass or other destructive vegetation on either side to catch the erring ball. I recollect that when I played at Woking, which was the first of our courses to be carved out of heathery country, those parallel and menacing lines seemed decidedly novel.

That was only twenty-five years ago. Seaside links had clumps of gorse or bushes here and there and there was of course plenty of bent grass on the sandhills, but there was no hard and fast middle way; if there were bents on the right there was open country on the left. As to inland courses, certainly I played, in the University match, on Wimbledon Common where there were some terribly narrow drives between gorse bushes but the three courses with which I was perhaps most familiar, had no rough of any kind. Two were on the Downs; the lovely springy turf stretched for miles on either hand and, apart from a chalk pit or two and a few hurdles, you could drive where you pleased under the vast dome of Heaven.

The third was of a type fortunately rarer. It was a flat, muddy Common, where the wretched golfers of Cambridge were condemned to play. The only trouble consisted in a few black and ill-scented ditches. Here lurked troops of black, ill-scented little boys who either recovered your ball from the water for a penny or, if they deemed it a more profitable speculation,

14

stamped the ball into the oozy mud and then, when you had passed on, stole it at their leisure.

I am not holding up these latter courses for admiration—far from it. I only use them as illustrations of the fact that clear-cut lines of rough have not always been with us. My experience is far too small for me to generalize but I did not see a course in America that did not have them. Nearly all our inland courses today have them. Only on some of the seaside courses do the old, more varied conditions exist. At St. Andrews, for instance, there is certainly a rather broken line of rough country to catch a slice on the way out but that is all. For the most part you are trying to avoid a particular bunker from the tee or obtain a certain strategic position for your next shot; you are not trying to go down a groove.

The same thing is true of Westward Ho! There are indeed plenty of tall and spiky rushes, but they are not, as it were, formed up in regular battalions but dotted irregularly here and there about the battle field. It would be possible to give other instances but I think, even on sensible courses, there is more definite rough than there used to be. Muirfield for instance, where Mr. Gardner fought his great fight with Mr. Tolley, resembles in this respect an inland course more than a links and even Sandwich has given us narrow alleys whereas before we wandered o'er the steppes.

It seems to me that golfing architects might sometimes with advantage compromise between the two systems more than they do at present. There is, I suppose, not much doubt that the parallel lines of rough make the better educational school because they insist on rigidly straight play. Indeed if St. Andrews does not turn out so many good golfers as it used to, it may be because the young golfers there, having too much license in the matter of erratic driving, do not sufficiently curb their traditional, loose, slashing style. On the other hand the sensation of being perpetually set in a framework of rough is a monotonous one and the golf tends to become monotonous.

It may be immoral, from the highest golfing point of view, that at St. Andrews a very wild hook may go scot free and a nearly perfect shot be trapped, but it is the endless variety of possible lines to every hole, changing with every little change of the wind, that make the unique charm of that great course. People often get annoyed with St. Andrews but they do not get bored with playing there. Where there is a definite fairway and definite rough, there is far less variety. Bang, bang, bang—right down the middle: that is the only game. There is little strategy of tactics: no flanking movements, only frontal attacks.

There should as a rule be two degrees of rough, purgatory and hell. It seems unfair but it is often the case that the man who goes one foot off the course lies in the grass just as thick and tangled as he who goes twenty or forty. The moderate sin should only entail purgatory—there should be some chance of a startling recovery. And apart from grounds of abstract justice, hunting for lost balls is a sad nuisance both to ourselves and those who play behind us. That is another reason for not having the rough one uniform "hell".

Indeed, I think, uniformity is a thing to be avoided. I think the hardest hole I ever knew—it was played with a gutty ball—was a three shotter in which the fairway ran absolutely straight from tee to hole. On each side of it was a ditch of uniform depth and beyond the ditch heather of a uniformly damnable character. There was one small bunker exactly in the middle of the course and just in front of the green and that was all. I think, as I said, that it was the hardest hole, and I am quite sure it was the dullest.

1923

Leaves From an
Old Diary

I feel sure that many golfers must have been studying with great and sentimental interest Mr. Keeler's "Autobiography of an Average Golfer," breathing once more the air of their youth in reading of his early struggles and recognizing long-lost clubs of their own that went by such names as the Hoylake cleek and the abbreviated brassie.

For myself, Mr. Keeler has sent me back to reading a golfing diary which I kept between 1899 and 1903. I cannot claim it as the history of the beginning of my game because I had at that date attained too much the same style of equable mediocrity as I now boast. It may some day be rather interesting as a scrap book since it has pasted into it various snapshots and photographs of groups, such as the two teams that played in the first England and Scotland match in 1902 and the menu that we all signed at the dinner afterwards. It also contains what is of very little interest to anyone else, a list of all the courses I had then played over and all the team matches I had played in. My total of courses amounted to about 130, twenty-one years ago, and as regards the number of team matches I really believe I must be the world's record-holder because by November, 1903, I had played in 103 of these contests and I have been adding pretty steadily to the number ever since.

But what I really claim for my diary is that it is rather an illuminating "human document." I kept it, if I may say so, very honestly. My praise of myself was sparing, my abuse often unsparing and, whatever I may have said in the heat of the moment, I did not write down that my conquerors were abominably lucky, laid me stymies, or jumped bunkers. Therefore, I think the record may be taken as a genuine one and it shows rather amusingly how true it is that "life is one d——d thing after another." Take for instance this series of entries: on the 2nd of January I say "Must learn to drive somehow. Am duck-

18

ing horribly." On the 6th things are clearly improving because we find "Driving fairly good." On the 15th "Driving really quite long" leads up to the highest possible praise on the 20th, "Driving very well." Alas, pride goes before a fall. On the very next day, the 21st, comes a defeat by a good many holes with this comment "Played very badly. Irritable and without pluck." Volumes could not say more. What a dreadfully unpleasant adversary I must have been that day.

In spite of that horrid crash, the driving seems to have come back and remained fairly good but now it was time that the putting should weaken. Coming events cast their shadows before, and on March 8th I was "playing moderately well but short game must be looked to." My premonition was only too correct. On the 10th the putting was "too vile for words" and three days later again came the climax "My putting this day reached a pitch of badness which may have been equalled but can never have been surpassed." In a week the short game had become "good" but to make up the long game is set down as "rather slicy." There is always a hitch.

Now let me cheer myself up by turning to a really cheerful page or two. It refers to a certain course in Wales and an old hunting ground of mine, in August and September, 1900. You can tell I was playing well by a mere glance at the page. First of all the writing is neat, tidy and legible. It is clear that I lingered gloatingly over portraying my matches. When, at other times, I was losing by 6 and 5, there is nothing but a hasty scrawl, as if I got a hateful duty over as soon as possible. Furthermore, on this nice, pretty page there is a whole series of scores set out and I find I only know what my score is when it is a fairly good one. There are three 75's in quick succession, two of them in a single day. Seventy-five was then the record (those were gutty days) and two of my rounds ended with a six, showing that the anxiety had proved something too much for me at the finish. Then at last on September 4th, a day to be marked with a white stone, comes this entry: "Beat So-and-So by 6 and 4. B. D. 71, beating record by 4 strokes — Nunc Dimittis!" Opposite is a photograph of the aforesaid

B. D. very obviously posing in an elegant attitude but supposed to be "at the top of his swing." Well, well, all things are
vanity but I always enjoy looking at that ingenious entry.

It is curious how, when one rereads such a record of old golf
matches, some are still quite fresh in the memory while others
are quite forgotten and the written work cannot bring them
back. It is not always the very good or very bad rounds that are
the most vivid. I see in my diary certain rounds that appear to
have left me perfectly self-satisfied and yet even the face of
my opponent has gone clean out of my head. On the other
hand here, over twenty years ago, I find a note of a few holes
played casually with a professional and this note, "He taught
me why I was standing crooked." It is rather an obscure statement about a purely practice round and yet it brings the whole
scene back with amazing vividness. I can remember the club I
was driving with, the very tee on which that professional told
me of my error, exactly what that error was, and the delicious
sensation of the drives that followed. Yet when a little later, I
find that I lost a match in a mildly-important tournament
through "very bad luck in driving into an inaccessible bunker
at the same home hole," I remember nothing whatever about
it. I like that little piece of flattery calling the bunker "inaccessible."

On the whole the sweets distinctly outnumber the bitters
in reading an old golfing diary. The "six downs" have lost their
smart but the "six ups" still give something of a grateful thrill.
I wish that I had never ceased to keep it but all my attempts to
start again have been dogged by bad luck. At the very moment I was going to buy a new book, I always seemed to lose
by 7 and 6 and really one could not inaugurate a diary with
"Driving ghastly, iron play ridiculous. Putting worse than
either."

"A Little Too Much Massy"

A little while ago I had what I had never had before in all my life, and I wish I had had it many years earlier—a formal lesson in golf from an illustrious teacher. Even so I had not meant to have it. I had been to see the great man about something else, and then, since there was half an hour to spare, I plucked up my courage and asked him to give me a lesson.

I was afraid—I blush to confess to such vanity—that I should by some unlucky chance, and inspired by his presence, hit the ball quite respectably well, and that he would thereupon declare that there was nothing the matter. These are words that fall like music on the ear when a periodical exploration is made by the family dentist, but this time, being conscious of a complexity of lethal diseases, I should have found them disappointing.

However, I had a coat that was too tight and a club I disliked, so that I was not without hope, and indeed, I need have had no fear for my first shots were as feeble, as crooked, and as bad in every conceivable way as I could possibly have wished. Each one illustrated a new and separate disease.

For a while my teacher only stood over me in brooding and contemplative silence. Then he took me by the shoulders and heaved me into an attitude that may have looked classical, but felt extremely uncomfortable. Then he gave up my feet as a bad job, and attacked a limb that I myself knew to be old and hardened in crime—namely, the right elbow. Having found out the criminal, he gave it no peace. Whenever, as is its beastly habit, it insisted on brandishing itself in the air, he remarked, "A little too much Massy again that time, Sir." This was certainly unjust to the great Frenchman, who had won the Open at Hoylake in 1907, but it had a most illuminating and beneficial effect.

I do not know whether I was the more impressed by the

astuteness of his comments, or by his kind and fatherly manner of nursing me back to a temporary convalescence. When a shot went wrong, and I exclaimed, almost in tears, "There, that wretched slice again," he would pat me—metaphorically—on the head and remark that the club has been swung properly, but that I had looked up just too soon.

Or he would say that it was not really a slice, but that I was "standing that way," and would demonstrate this comforting theory by putting his own feet into my footprints. Or, again, when I said in despair, "Oh! but I've often tried that and all that happens is ect.," he just let me talk, and then invented some beautiful explanation that should hearten me to try the particular experiment again. He was so soothing and so ingenious, and yet stuck so tenaciously to the main issue, discarding all minor points, that in about a quarter of an hour he had me lashing and slashing at the ball with confidence, and sending it, moreover, a very tolerable distance.

There have been relapses since, alas! I cannot, fortunately for him, for he would find me a sad bore, go and live on his doorstep, under his fatherly eye. But he gave me at least some exquisite moments, and I am still moderately full of faith.

What a hard life that great man must lead. I cannot doubt, as I said, that he found me a bore, but he only suffered me for half an hour, and he has to do the same sort of thing sometimes for several hours a day. Moreover, I cannot help thinking that some of his pupils are more tedious even than I was, for I did hit the ball at last, and some of them, whatever they may do in the next world, will never hit it in this. They are older than I am, their figures are more prohibitively convex. He tees up a row of balls for them, and they topple them along the ground. He picks up the balls, and tees them again, and they topple them once more, and he will go on teeing them with perfect suavity, and they will go on toppling them with perfect futility till the end of time. What a life!

And yet he remains philosophic and even serene. Surely there is lost in him the finest schoolmaster that ever lived.

Atupsia

The word at the head of this article will not, I believe, be found in any dictionary, but it is compounded on the best philological principles for all that. It is derived from that old friend—or enemy—of our learning-Latin school days. *Tupto* "I strike," and the alpha in front of it, is called, if I remember rightly, "alpha privative" and means roughly speaking that you can't do it. Therefore Atupsia is the name of a rare and dreadful golfing disease and means that you can't strike the ball.

"Rare?" you may say, "surely not! It is my commonest disease in all golf."

But I do not mean that kind. I am not thinking of topping or slicing or even of missing the globe. Atupsia is a nervous disease which, as it were, petrifies the club in your grasp and makes you powerless. The name was coined by Mr. Horace Hutchinson for the case of a friend of his and mine, a very famous cricketer and racket player who was suddenly struck down. He was quite a good golfer but one day he got his club up in the top of the swing and no power on earth could get it down again. Nor did he recover for quite a long time.

I never saw him in the throes but I have seen another sufferer and it really was a painful sight. This patient, who had taught himself a very careful and laborious full swing, would take the club up and then it just stuck. He tugged and wrenched at it like a man in a bad temper pulling at a bell rope. Sometimes it came down a little way and stuck again. Sometimes it did actually get down to the ball but slowly and at so odd an angle that the shot was predoomed to utter failure. At other times he would have, so to speak, to lift it down and begin all over again. This sufferer never did recover, though he had convalescent intervals and not being very young, ultimately gave up the game altogether.

Another form of the disease consists in getting the club stuck behind the ball and being unable to begin the swing at all. I knew one golfer who caught it very badly. He could waggle freely enough but once he had put the club down behind the ball he was impotent. So he went to a suggestion doctor who hypnotized him and told him to take the first train down to his golf club, tee half a dozen balls and hit them. He duly obeyed orders and off were the six balls, far and sure down the fairway. Afterwards he had relapses and had to be treated again but in the end he recovered.

That was an aggravated case but I suppose most of us have had the disease for a few holes in a mild form. At first sight it might appear rather beneficial than otherwise since most people snatch back the club all too quickly and a short compulsory pause might do them good. I do not think that this is sound reasoning, however, because that feeling of not being able to start when we want to takes all rhythm out of the stroke, and rhythm is just about the most important thing in the world in starting the swing.

Once the club gets struck we feel that we have to tear it away with an effort and get "snatchier" than ever. Unless I am mistaken Mr. Walter Travis used at one time—perhaps he does it still—to refrain from grounding his club behind the ball or at any rate grounded it very lightly indeed. That great golfer never did anything, I am sure, without a reason, and I am equally sure he never suffered from Atupsia.

On the putting green partial Atupsia is a very common disease indeed. We can see victims on any course and any day. The attack comes on after we have soled our club behind the ball and have taken that last glance at the hole. Suddenly we feel that it cannot be a final glance; we must have one more and yet another. Our head goes up and down, up and down and all the while our knees bend a little more and we crouch yet a little closer to the ground. Finally when we make up what we are pleased to call our minds to strike, we have got into the attitude of a trussed fowl. We are so dazed and cramped that it is ten to one the ball finishes contemptibly short of the hole.

The caddies at Westward Ho! who are shrewd judges of the game, have a Devonshire word which well describes what a stroke at golf should be—"suent." They will talk of a man hitting the ball "suently," which means something like rhythmically; it indicates that each part of the swing followed the preceding part smoothly and at the proper time. There is nothing in which we ought to be more "suent" than in putting, but we very seldom are so, and the hitch often comes with the last look at the hole.

Some of the best and most rhythmic putters dispense entirely with that last look. They take their looks before they sole the putter behind the ball. Once they have soled their putter, they simply putt. Mr. John Low, a graceful putter if there ever was one, has this gift to perfection, and I have observed that our current amateur champion, Mr. Holderness, dramatically improved his putting when he gave up that last look. Cutting it out, of course, is a difficult business. I confess to having tried without success even though I firmly believe we shall putt better without it.

I do not know if prolonged waggling can be described as a form of Atupsia, but it certainly belongs to the same family of diseases. The waggle excessive attacks us as a rule in some tight corner when we are strung up and anxious. Even in a friendly match when we do not care two pence about the outcome, we can be suddenly overcome by thinking too precisely about some particular point of style. Just as we are going to hit, our mind wanders for a moment. We say to ourselves: "What the devil must I remember? Is it my stiff left arm or my stiff right knee or my—etc., etc." And in that one fatal moment we succumb. A very famous golfer indeed, Sandy Herd, did it all the time, something on the order of eight to thirteen waggles per stroke. And he won the Open championship with all those waggles too. But he was able to make them part of his game. Some facetious spectator is reputed to have said to him: "You take a damned long time to hit the ball." "Yes, but I hit it damned well when I do," was his reply, and he did.

St. Andrews in August

I have just finished a round at St. Andrews with a feeling of profound thankfulness for not having committed infanticide. From the last tee my ball leaped lightly over the left ear of a small and day-dreaming boy who was walking along the road that crosses the links and leads to the shore. All day long there is a procession along it of motor cars, perambulators, children and old ladies and the golfer, learning perforce to be callous, drives over, round, or through them from the first and from the last tees. Mr. Horton in his box periodically shouts "Fore" at the people in a voice of thunder or rather he makes some horrific sound with no distinguishable consonants in it, but nobody pays any attention and, which is more surprising, nobody is killed.

St. Andrews in August is distinctly different from St. Andrews in September. September is the month of the public vase and the Medal when "Everybody as is anybody" feels bound to come here and meets all the golfers one ever knew in the clubroom. In August there are plenty of members here, but it is preeminently the season of the golfing day-tripper from Edinburgh, from Glasgow, from all over the place. Most of them play golf and all of them putt. Excluding the ladies' club putting course which is select and genteel, where you must be accompanied by a member and must play with a putter of wood on the sacred turf; excluding also the children's links on the far side of the road by the seventeenth green; there are three public putting courses.

You pay two pence or a penny. You hire a putter, if you need one, and a ball from which the vestiges of paint have long since vanished, and you putt. These greens are just outside the white railing between the shore on one side and the fairway to the first hole on the other. One of them is in considerable peril from the sliced drives from the first tee, and I apprehend that on this one you only pay a penny, because of the enhanced risk to your life. The greens are not very good (how could they be with the constant tramping?), but they are very amusing and there is something extraordinarily friendly and jolly about the whole performance. You feel that putting is not the solemn and agonizing business that you have so often imagined it, but a popular pastime with vast scope for rollicking humour, like going on a roller-coaster at Coney Island.

Of course, there is plenty of solemn golf too. At this present moment there is a big open tournament on the Eden course with so many entries that the qualifying rounds take two days. In it are playing such well known golfers as Mr. de Montmorency and Mr. John Caven, both of whom have played for Britain against America, and a host of those artisan golfers with whom Scotland abounds—golfers who from lack of time and means seldom go far from their home courses but who have all the dash and style of the professional and want only something of his steadiness and experience. There are big crowds watching the play, for the Scots never tire of watching golf, but this does not seem to diminish by a single man, woman or child the crowd that is playing on the Old Course and on the New. They were hard at it when I looked out of my bedroom window at 8 o'clock this morning and they will still be hard at it when in a few minutes I strike across the edge of the last green to dress for my dinner at 8 o'clock in the evening. And nearly every match is a four ball match because it takes three hours to get round and to play a single is to become a martyr to impatience on every tee.

Nothing demonstrates so well the unique fascination of St. Andrews as the fact that golfers who might go anywhere else come here year after year and gladly suffer all the slowness and all the inconveniences in order to play on the Old Course. That is the magnet. The New Course is a very fine one. If it were anywhere else in the world except under the shadow of the Old, it would be very famous. It is even argued that judged by orthodox standards of architecture it is as good as the Old. Yet everybody wants to get a place in the ballot for starting times on the Old and nobody but regards the New as a *pis aller*. The Calcutta Cup foursome tournament is played on the New Course. Yet I remember that two years ago, not one single player took the trouble to go for a preliminary round of exploration on the New. They just played it "blind" because they would not spare one precious moment from the delights of the Old. There is nothing like it anywhere else, though I am sure I cannot explain why. The best reason I know is George Duncan's that "You can play a d——d good shot there and find the ball in a d——d bad place!"

Strange Clubs

It chanced the other day that a friend asked me to play golf, and I replied that my clubs were inaccessible, but I would try to play him with a set made up of old throw-aways. An eminent person who was standing near thereupon remarked: "Do you have to have your own? Does it make any difference?" I looked at him doubtfully for a moment—half suspecting an insult. I concluded that he spoke in perfect innocence. What is more, I am not sure that his question was not a very sensible one. Does it really make so very much difference?

In this particular case it made the difference—and a very considerable difference it is—that I hit the ball. But, of course, these clubs were not really strangers: they were only discarded members of my family of clubs. One of them, indeed, had been discarded for no fault of his own, but because he had had, some years ago, a very severe operation. A golfing surgeon had taken bits of his inside out, stuck them together with glue, put them back, and bound them up. Binding right down to the head always spoils a club's looks sadly, giving a high-shoul-dered almost humpbacked air, and so, since this one had at once grown frail and ugly, I put him away.

This was the club that behaved so nobly. He began with the most glorious, wholehearted hook which just missed a horse and hit a man, and never fell away from this high standard. I was a little impressed by the good behavior of the putter, since fresh putters always flatter to deceive, and as to the mashie (5 iron), one of a particular brand is much like another; but that this aged, broken-down pensioner of wood should play up in this way was a genuine surprise. He pretends he is A1 when nobody with that amount of glue in his inside can really be better than C3. He will no doubt resort to lies to get back to the front and the trenches. I shall have to take him back into my bag. However much I may nurse him by never letting him hit anything but a teed ball, he will finally be broken in my service, preferring death in the field to dishonour in the cupboard.

These clubs, which are at least of the weight and lie that their owner once liked, should not long feel unfamiliar, but a perfectly strange set belonging to someone else, or even an assortment chosen from several bags, will sometimes do wonders. It is part of golfing history that the late Douglas Rolland played one of his most brilliant rounds with a scratch set casually picked up in the shop. He had, too, on that occasion arrived on the course, through some mischance, in a stiff white shirt and boots with no nails.

But Rolland had a genius for golf that has never been surpassed, and ordinary people cannot be judged by his standard. I have, however, a pleasing recollection of a much humbler fear. I played in a coat far too tight, heavily swathed into the bargain in woolly waistcoats, with somebody else's clubs, which were as unlike my own as chalk is unlike cheese; and I won a foursome by many holes. It is but honest to add that the other three players were all, if I remember rightly, aldermen of the London Country Council.

Alderman apart, the phenomenon is capable of explanation. When, some years ago, I was suddenly thrust on to a horse, after many years' absence from the saddle, I did not waste much time on thinking whether my back was looking like what my chest ought to be: I merely tried to adhere to that horse as it scoured at will the Macedonian plain.

Similarly, when we have thrust into our hands a strange club, we do not think about style: we try simply to hit the ball. If, and when, we succeed we do not know why, and so we go on carefully, prayerfully thumping. It is only when the club begins to feel familiar that the bacillus of thought has a chance of entering into us.

Some twenty-five years ago Mr. Guy Ellis, when at his best—and how good that best was, comparatively few people now realize—played three rounds a day at St. Andrews for several weeks on end. His explanation of his consistently good golf was that he played each round with a different set of clubs, since by this device "it was impossible to get stale." The recipe appears an extravagant one, but it is founded on some understanding, for if you have to concentrate your mind on a strange club you have neither time to get bored nor to study fatuous and imaginary differences in your own sensations.

Generally speaking, however, most of us would probably not do much worse than usual with the other fellow's clubs. It is not that we should play well—far from it—but in considering the question, we assume erroneously that we play well with our own. And this, perhaps, was what that eminent person had in mind when he asked his question with so guileless and inscrutable an air.

The Pupil

I have just been spending an amusing and instructive half hour at the "Golf Week" at Harrods, which is one of our largest London stores. There were assembled all the greatest professional lights, Vardon, Taylor, Herd, Duncan, Mitchell and several slightly less resplendent luminaries, ready to sell clubs or to give lessons to anybody that came along. For this purpose, there were several large nets, there was a putting green rug with a real hole and a bunker of most undeniable sand.

I must say I always admire the man or the woman—the women are generally the braver of the two—who takes a lesson in public in this way. I always feel rather ashamed of myself when I stand and watch them, as if I were one of those intrusive persons who *will* look over the shoulder of a wretched landscape painter. However I always manage to stifle my scruples.

This time when I got there, business was rather slack. There was but one brave man having a lesson—in iron play from its acknowledged master J. H. Taylor.

"You ought to go and look at J. H. putting the half-Nelson on him" said one of the other professionals.

It was an apt description for Taylor had seized his pupil in an iron grip and was bending him into excruciating attitudes that he had never dreamed of. The arms and limbs of the two became so inextricably involved that they looked like the statue of Laocoon.

At intervals Taylor would show his victim how to play an iron shot. Crash! down came the club. Pieces came out of the mat on which the ball was teed, the ground rocked, the net quivered. And then came the imitation. It was really instructive for it showed how badly we imitate the great iron players. It was nothing in the world but a stiff jab.

"No, no sir," cried J. H. in an agony. "You're too stiff, too stiff. Flexible—be more flexible. Don't use your right hand as if you were the heavyweight champion."

I never before realized how great yet how subtle a difference there is between the firm iron shot of the good golfer and its counterfeit by the bad one. All that the poor pupil could do was make his wrists as stiff as pokers and stop the club with a quiver and a jerk.

There was another interesting thing about this pupil. He was a socketer, a really wicked, confirmed socketer. Most of us have a slight attack of this dread disease now and again and cannot quite make out why the ball should suddenly fly to the right leaving that horrible tell-tale white mark on the heel.

Well, here was a socketer so bad that one could see exactly why and how he did it. He took the club back, slowly and laboriously, as if it weighed a ton, with a vice-like grip of the right hand. During this process he gradually accumulated all his weight onto his left foot, so that his left knee was bent far out toward the ball, and his head was thrust forward till it was nearly over the ball. Then suddenly and viciously he let fly that knockout punch with the right hand.

The result was inevitable. The left knee had no time to get back to its original position and down came the club in an outward direction right on top of the ball. As Taylor remarked afterward almost pathetically. "Where else could he hit it except on the heel?"

The next time I have a fit of socketing, I am going to call up a mental picture of that pupil and try to look just as unlike it as I possibly can. To know how to socket is some way on the road to knowing how to avoid it, and he was the best socketer I ever saw.

To Look or
Not to Look

Some day, no doubt, a prophet will arise, who will traverse the country up and down, like a devouring flame, bearing a banner on which are inscribed the words, "Take your eye off the ball." In his iconoclastic zeal, he will seek out and destroy all the beautiful photographs of Taylor, which show that great man still staring venomously at the ground after the ball had departed. And, since it does not really matter much what you tell golfers to do, so long as they believe in you, he will at first bring new hope and gladness to many stricken bosoms. His end is almost certain. He will be lynched by a mob of infuriated socketers and toppers. I suppose he will deserve it, and yet I am not sure. There may be something to be said for him. To keep the eye on the ball is, of course, extremely important, but I sometimes think people have protested too much about it. There may be said to be two schools of thought on the subject. One regards the taking of the eye off the ball as an original sin, which can be dealt with only by the direct method, namely, by keeping the eye on the ball. The other believes that it is not a sin on its own account at all, but is caused by some antecedent crime, committed in an earlier part of the swing, and that, therefore, the direct method of cure is of no use at all.

Of this latter school, George Duncan is one of the acknowledged leaders. He told me once that he did not believe that ever in his life had he taken his eye off the ball, unless he had first done something wrong in his back swing, which caused his eye to misbehave. Of the direct school, I cannot instance any famous member. I know a great many people who say, "My dear fellow, nothing matters a hang as long as you look at the ball," but fame has never yet come their way. I think there must be a little something else that does matter.

As regards full shots, I am to a great extent a believer in

34

Duncan's precept. I think nine times out of ten, the poor in-nocent eye would like to be virtuous, but it is simply forced off the ball by a vicious, ill-controlled body. When it comes to the shorter shots, the eye is not, I fancy, so innocent and is quite capable of moving and wandering away on its own ac-count. I certainly do believe that in driving it is possible to harm yourself to look too hard at the ball. I know it is an axiom of the great Braid's that to insist too much on the eye on the ball is to cramp the follow through, and this was brought home to me the other day by a personal experience.

My driving was not so bad, but I had a thoroughly uncom-fortable sensation that my eye was being forced away from the ball with a jerk just a fraction of a second too soon. The more I tried to see that ball, the more uncomfortable I felt. At last I determined on a new and perilous course of action. I decided that this confounded eye of mine, the moment it had seen the ball struck, was not to try to stay still or to look at the ground a la Taylor. Rather my head was to turn easily and smoothly round and my eye was to gaze rapturously at the horizon.

This seemed a desperate venture, but it succeeded. My fol-low through was a thing of freedom and job. There was a deli-cious sensation of the right shoulder really doing its share of the work, and the feeling of constraint had disappeared. I was neither conscious or unconscious of seeing the ball as I hit it. I just did not care.

I am far from alleging that I improved my hitting for the moment by taking my eye off the ball. No doubt I was in fact seeing the ball much more clearly at the critical moment than I had been before. The explanation is simply that by thinking too hard about keeping one's eye on the ball, one can get oneself into so thoroughly strained, tautened and muscle-bound a condition that a free swing is in the highest degree improbable.

To keep the eye gazing too fiercely on the ground after the ball has sped away has a tendency to check that free move-ment of the right shoulder, which is one of the most delight-ful sensations produced by a perfectly-timed drive. At the same time this is a cure which must be used most sparingly. It is all very well for the head to turn round a little in order to finish out the swing, but for heaven's sake, do not let it jump up, for that is fatal.

When it comes to short pitches and putts these perilous observations have, I think, no application, for it is then hardly possible to keep the eye too fiercely on the ball. Merely to determine to keep the eye there may not, however, be the best means to attaining that end. I have a friend, an eminent lawyer, who has taken an immense amount of thought about his putting and has been well repaid for doing so. According to him the player takes his eye off the ball in putting for a particular psychological reason. Just before he swings his club back, he takes a final look at the hole. Therefore, the last mental picture that has possession of his mind before the stroke is that of the hole, with the fatal result that the eye looks up too soon toward the hole.

The way to cure this, so declares my friend, is to put into the mind some picture, still later in point of time than that of the hole. Consequently the very last thing that he tries to think of is the ground three or four inches in front of the ball, and he looks at nothing else until he has seen his club come through on to that spot of turf. I am not prepared to guarantee a cure from this patent medicine, but I can guarantee the original patentee as a very fine putter.

The Ordeal of Waiting

In just a fortnight's time from the day on which I write these lines, I shall be starting north, probably in exuberant spirits, for a week at St. Andrews. I cannot look into the future and say whether it will be hot or cold or whether I shall hook or slice, but one thing I can prophesy with the utmost exactitude: each round that I play on the classic Old Course will take me, almost to the minute, three hours.

It does not matter who leads the field or who plays immediately in front of you; it may be Vardon, Braid and Taylor or it may be two old ladies and a small boy. When St. Andrews is full in holiday time, the pace of the green is always the same. Sometimes you may get to the turn in an hour and a quarter and think you are going to beat the record—for speed, not strokes. It is the vainest delusion, for you will certainly have to wait thirty-five minutes on the tee at the notorious eleventh. Conversely, if you go out more slowly than usual you will come home, comparatively speaking, like a streak of lightning. The time will be always the same in the end and that fact is the saving of the situation. You are so entirely reconciled beforehand to waiting that you do not feel even inclined to lose your temper. St. Andrews would not be St. Andrews without it.

The real bitterness of waiting, the thing that makes the impatient man dance with impotent rage is the thought of what might have been. If only you had not stopped to talk to Jones for two minutes about something of no importance; if only you had not forgotten your pipe and run back for it, you would not have got behind those two old gentlemen, as to whom you have to look at the hedge in the background to swear that they are moving, and you would have been striding along and playing, as you feel sure, beautifully.

As it is, "Confound you, Sir," you shout under your breath in a furious whisper, "Do get on. That's twelve waggles I've counted. Hit the ball, Sir, can't you. Good Heavens, man, you need n't wait. You couldn't get up from that distance if you tried for a hundred years"—and so on.

After a few holes, one of the old gentlemen appears to be looking for his ball. Here is a Heaven-sent opportunity. You take up your club, you are just going to play and then, in the nick of time, he has found his ball. With a bitter curse you hurl the club into your bag. You might have known he never would lose his ball—he could not hit it far enough to send it out of sight.

Exactly how infuriating you find these two old gentlemen depends on a variety of circumstances but chiefly on whether or not you are winning your match. Perhaps I should not say "you." It is too personal and you of course are always in an angelic temper, but look at A and B—there on the fourteenth tee with two other couples waiting in front of them to play that short hole over the water jump. A is three up with five to play. He accepts the situation philosophically, sits down, lights his pipe and inquires in a friendly manner as to the state of the other players' matches.

B, on the other hand, cannot sit still but struts and fumes, ever and anon taking a pinch of sand out of the box and then, when he finds it becoming unpleasantly hot in his hand, casting it peevishly from him. A long wait is terribly hard to bear when our fortunes are at their lowest.

There is one man that I am sure we must all often have felt sorry for and that is the ordinary mortal of the rank and file who is drawn with some stars in a competition. He always has to wait for the crowd to get out of his way and the crowd never by any chance waits for him. Even when both are entitled to the rank of stars, one of them sometimes has a poor time of it.

There was a famous occasion at the Open Championship at St. Andrews in 1900 when Harry Vardon, the reigning Open Champion, and Mr. Hilton, the reigning amateur, were drawn together. Mr Hilton gives an amusing account of it in his book of reminiscences. "The crowd lined up behind Vardon's ball, leaving me a solid phalanx of spectators to play over. I couldn't possibly play; there did not seem to be anyone who would take on him the responsibility of informing the crowd of the situation and I certainly did not feel equal to it myself. I had done enough work of that description for one day, so I calmly sat down beside my ball and awaited developments. The fact is, I was lost."

Not unlike this occasion was one at Prestwick when Vardon and Taylor were drawn together and were leading the field. On that occasion a friend of mine who was helping to shepherd the crowd, tried to make room for the protagonists with the usual of "Players please!" He received from a burly Scottish miner the answer "Players be d———d. We've come here to see." Sublime illogicality could go no further.

1924

The Dun and the Dowie

I have just come back from watching the Oxford and Cambridge match at Hoylake in which an American golfer greatly distinguished himself. I call Mr. Pulling an American golfer because he was at Princeton and learned his golf there, although he is a British citizen and served in our navy in the war. He had a fine match with another young giant, Mr. Stephenson, the Oxford football player, and was one down at the end of twenty-seven holes. Then he came away with such golf as the oldest inhabitant had never seen. His first six holes coming home were 3, 3, 3, 2, 4, 4. This with the wind as it was, represented four birdies and two pars. It is not surprising that at the end of these six he had won his match.

This, however, is by the way. Hoylake was interested in the University match but still more interested in the new holes that had just been built and the changes that had been made in some of the old ones. I never heard so much talk about the rights and wrongs of bunkers in all my life, and indeed one or two of these changes are something more than local matters, not only because Hoylake is a classic course, but because the principles underlying them seem to go to the root of the whole architectural business. The question is this—When a hole has a very distinct character of its own and a long tradition into the bargain, is it best to leave it alone, or should it be "improved" so as to conform to the most fashionable standard of modern architecture?

I will try to describe two of the holes briefly and I hope intelligently. Both have famous names and are called after departed Scottish heroes. The seventh is the Dowie and the sixteenth is the Dun and they are always called by their names and not their numbers. The Dowie was once profanely described to me by Mr. Laidlay as "the kind of hole you would expect to find on Clapham Common," and it is quite unique.

It is about 170 yards long and the green is the queerest little triangle of turf. On its left edge is a grass bank called in Cheshire a "cop," and over the bank is out of bounds. The righthand edge is guarded by an irregular grassy dip, a few inches deep and a very few inches wide which looks like an intoxicated furrow. In front of the green is a rather anemic patch of bushes. To the right is a clear space of grass. To hit a ball right up to this pin with that out of bounds so perilously close has always been a feat of great daring. Consequently the usual method has been to push the tee shot out to the right and then play a running-up shot through the grassy gutter and hope for the best. It may not sound a very good hole as I describe it, but on the whole it repaid good play and it was interesting because there was nothing else like it in the world.

Now two bunkers, one beyond on the other, have been cut not far from the right-hand edge of the green. The running shot from the right is still possible, but to get the position for it is far more difficult. Theoretically those bunkers are all right and the old empty space was quite wrong. They demand a more accurate tee shot, they do something towards equalizing the punishment for slicing and hooking, they penalize the player of a nondescript scuffling approach and glorify the already glorious person who can go the whole way in the air and dead straight. Only they tend to turn the Dowie merely into the seventh hole.

Now for the Dun. This is a long hole of nearer 500 than 400 yards. An out-of-bounds territory eats its way into the fairway on the right and bang across the front of the green—I speak of the past in the present tense—is a deep, wide cross bunker. The very long hitter takes his life in his hands, cuts off the biggest chunk of out of bounds he dares, just carries the cross bunker and so is magnificently home, or magnificently trapped. The ordinary person goes cautiously round and pitches home in three—still over that cross bunker, which always gives him a nervous tremor.

That is what used to happen, but then people began to get sorry for that big hitter and say that it was hard on him if he just got trapped with a great and daring second. So the cross bunker has been filled up and a line of pots placed across the course considerably nearer the tee. Everybody is supposed to be happier. The young slasher can slash home and everyone else can pitch home without being worried by that cross bunker. And to my thinking the whole character of the hole has gone. That deep, uncompromising trench frightened everyone: the new pots frighten no one. What was a little "unfairness" now and then compared to the ancient terror and the ancient splendor? As long as the old cross bunker was there, every newcomer to Hoylake was shown the spot from which in the gutty days Mr. John Ball played his most historic shot.

It was the final of the 1894 Championship and Mr. Ball was one down with three to go—the Dun was the 16th in those days—although Mr. Ball had once been four up. Mr. Ball's adversary, Mr. S. Mure Fergusson, played safely for a five. He himself hesitated for a moment then took his brassie (2 wood) and hit a tremendous shot. The ball carried the cross bunker by inches and lay close to the hole. He got his four and won the match at the last hole. Many people will doubtless get up to that green with their seconds in future Championships, but the supreme risk, the chance of "hard luck" is gone and with it the supreme glory.

I admit that I am a conservative. I sometimes dislike changes for their own sake but I do also think that character is what we want more than anything else in a golfing hole. There is an old story of a lady's singing being praised on the ground that she "had so much taste" to which a sardonic wit added "and all of it so bad." A golfing hole, the character of which is all bad had better be abolished, but a hole with a great deal of character and just a little badness is worth a hundred of the blameless creations of orthodox architecture.

To take an extreme example, every one who has ever been there remembers the first and last holes at St. Andrews. In each case the player has a whole parish of empty turf into which to drive with impunity. Only, a prodigious slice will land him in the one case on the seashore, in the other in the window of some innocent citizen's house. Practically speaking, there is so much room that the tee shot can come to no harm. It is beyond question that both these drives could be made much more interesting and difficult, regarded in the abstract, by a few bunkers. It is equally beyond question that nobody but a Goth and a Vandal would propose to cut them there. St. Andrews is an extreme case, but only in this that it belongs to the whole world. Everyone of us holds in his heart some one course that is to him as St. Andrews, so that he would not lightly change it and I maintain that kept within limits there is a reasonable and proper reluctance.

I suppose the ground at Yonkers on which the "Apple-tree Gang" first played is now no longer a course, but if it were and if the holes would be better holes with fewer apple trees, would it not yet be a sin to cut down the smallest tree? The eighteenth hole at The Country Club is played, if I remember rightly, over the rather dreary waste of a polo ground until the bunker just in front of the green is reached. I would keep it thus void of bunkers—polo or no polo—not because it is a great hole, which it is not, but because it is the hole at which Francis Ouimet first made a tie with Vardon and Ray and then beat them. Perhaps I am a shameful sentimentalist, but I cannot help it.

Bad Useful Golf

I do not know what anonymous genius invented the expression "Good useless golf," but he said in three words what we most of us say in far too many when we have just lost a match. Indeed, I fancy that he said it, not with any conscious desire of turning a phrase, but in the hope of checking a flood of lamentable explanation that did not interest him.

Those three words generally imply an essential futility in the neighborhood of the green and an incapacity to take chances. We may spurt, but we always wait just too long before doing so. We are never beaten by much, but we are always beaten.

The opposite of this admirable phrase is less often heard, and yet "bad useful golf" conveys just as pithily and distinctly a common state of affairs. No single tee shot is clearly hit: the ball is, as a rule, smothered or half-topped, and has a touch of slice on it, and yet it always evades the bunker by inches. The iron shots are poor things, mistimed and pushed out; still they scramble onto the green somehow; generally by means of a lucky kick. And the putting and chipping from off the edge of the green are, of course, beyond reproach. The doubtful putts are all holed, and two or three long ones stagger into the cup.

In fact, our game is a long drawn out series of "two of those and one of them" followed by a "plop" or "plunk"—or any other agreeable onomatopoeic word—against the back of the tin, the whole making up what is humorously called a par four. Par indeed! And yet a succession of such fours are undeniably and horribly useful, not merely for their intrinsic merits, such as they are, but because they are apt to impair the enemy's courage more effectually than the most flawless golf.

I played just such a round only the other day, and my feelings alternated throughout between an impish glee and utter shame. I was the more ashamed because my young adversary bore it all, not merely with a stoical courtesy but with a smiling face, whereas I knew that, had we changed places, I should have been either tearful, or apoplectic, or both.

If this bad useful golf is to be as useful as possible we should observe certain rules of conduct. We should accept it for what it is, and not try for the moment to improve upon it. We should say with somebody in the Battle of Lake Regillus, "The gods, who live forever, are on our side today," and leave the matter in their hands accordingly. If we take thought about the drives, they may possibly go a little farther, but they will lose their invulnerable quality. The ball will then go "plop" into the bunker, not into the hole. The kind of golf we are playing may be of a very poor kind, but it is better than none at all, and we must recognize this as quickly as possible.

On the other hand we must also recognize the fact that it will not happen next time and, before we play again, we must physic ourselves, in a golfing sense, severely. There is only the difference of about a quarter of an inch on the putting green between the "bad useful" and the "bad useless," which is the lowest stage of all.

Although we acknowledge in our inmost hearts that we are for this one round under heavenly protection, we must never say so aloud; no, not even, if we follow what we say with some superstitious safeguard such as "knock on wood." We must never assert the plain truth of the matter: that it makes no difference how we stroke the ball since a pitch is sure to be close and a putt sure to go in. The Gods of Golf simply will not tolerate any impiety. To say "I have been putting well" is blasphemous; "I am putting well" is fatal.

The other day I was playing in a friendly team match, and at luncheon one of the other side, who had won his single, explained his victory by the statement that he was not much good at anything else, but he *could* hole putts. He said this with the utmost modesty; it was in truth not a boast but an apology, and yet I could not help feeling that here was a man defying lightning. When I found that he was to be one of my opponents in the foursomes after lunch, my hopes rose high, nor were they disappointed. The poor soul could hardly ever lay the ball dead. It was a truly pathetic sight. His partner became infected with the same microbe. Worse, neither could hole it even when it was dead. It was an awful warning.

In Mr. Eric Parker's Eton Anthology, there is a pleasant story of a member of the cricket eleven who declared that he was put out because he omitted some particular, superstitious formula of his before the ball was pitched. Mr. R. A. H. Mitchell replied—and one can hear the uncompromising tone in which he said it—"You'll be put out with that stroke no matter what you do."

That, no doubt, represents the braver and more common-sense view, but for myself I prefer to remain a slave to my own heathenish beliefs. Indeed, this article is only a humble thanks-giving to the hidden powers that befriended me last week, and a plea for further favors on the next occasion—it will come all too soon—when I am driving like an old lady and pitching like a small child.

A Game With
Mr. Ball

John Ball was the first amateur and first Englishman to win the British Open,
which he did in 1890. He won eight British Amateur titles. He is considered
to be the greatest British amateur golfer of all time.

I had a few days ago a great pleasure which I had not enjoyed
for a long time, namely a game with Mr. John Ball over his
own Hoylake. On this particular occasion he was not at his
best, yet he has been playing finely. Two or three days before,
at St. Anne's in Lancashire, a long punishing course, he had
played against the leader of the Oxford and Cambridge golfing society side and murdered him to the tune of 5 and 3. A
little while before that he had played the Oxford captain in a
match at Hoylake and after being five up at the eighth hole,
had relented a little in the old kind-hearted, masterful way to
win just at that most convenient hole, nearest to the clubhouse, the sixteenth. On the day of our game he had break-
fasted about half-past seven in the morning in order to motor
from Wales to Hoylake—and he is sixty-one. Really he is a
very wonderful man.

Moreover he is almost if not quite as good to look at as he
has been any time these last six and forty years—he was in the
prize test in the Open Championship when he was fifteen.
Some of the length and sting have naturally departed: he can
no longer play that tremendous forcing cleek (2 iron) shot
that sent the ball fizzing through the wind just at the height of
a man's head. But even now no man swings the club more
easily nor has a freer, bigger turn of the hips.

He provides an object lesson in the matchless value of style.
How many of the punchers and sloggers of today will be able
to hit the ball as he does when they are fifty-one to say nothing of sixty-one? Whenever I see either Mr. Ball or Mr. Bobby
Jones play, each of them reminds me of the other. Each has

the turning movement of the body to perfection and seems to play every shot by means of it, regulating it according to the length of the shot. In each case one forgets about the hands and the arms: the man swings his body rhythmically and truly and the body passes on the movement to the club. It appears impossible that that beautifully oiled piece of machinery should ever get out of order and in fact it seldom does.

Mr. Ball still goes perfectly straight down the middle of the course and is rather indignant when he observes some young slasher putting his tee shot into the rough and then recovering by means of a huge heave with a lofted iron. I think he would like all the rough to be a matted jungle and all the bunkers twenty feet deep with perpendicular sides.

Mr. Ball has a sovereign and supreme contempt for many of the small pot-bunkers which we see dotted about modern courses, and shows it by the masterly ease with which he flicks the ball out of them. At the second hole at Hoylake the other day he was trapped in one of the new pot bunkers to the right of the green and laid a pitch and run shot within six feet of the hole exactly as if he were playing off a flat piece of turf. And he did it not with a mashie niblick (7 iron), or even a mashie (5 iron), but with a club with a straight face that looked like a midiron (3 iron). And then when later on we came to the thirteenth, a short hole of 157 yards called the Rushes, he used that same straight-faced club again from the tee. The wind was behind us, the hole cut very near the copbunker. I took a tee and a lofted mashie and with much pains and labor contrived to make the ball sit on the green; Mr. Ball could get his ball higher into the air than mine and make it stop quicker by playing off the bare turf with a straight-faced club.

That shot of his has always been a heart-break and a mystery. How on earth does he do it and what on earth would happen if one day he really did play a stroke with a much laid back club? The nearest approach to an answer was provided back in the 1890s, when Mr. Ball and Mr. Leslie Balfour Melville met in a famous championship final at St. Andrews. They went to the nineteenth hole and both had to play short of the Burn in two. Mr. Balfour Melville pitched safely over but when Mr. Ball played his shot there came a smothered groan of horror. He had pitched the ball almost straight up into the air and it came almost straight down again, into the fatal waters of the Burn. Some malignant demon had tempted him to take a mashie which he hardly ever used in place of his trusty midiron. I doubt whether he has ever used that mashie or any other really lofted club more than half a dozen times since.

When sometimes I am in a mood to be a praiser of past times, I wonder whether the elder players had not more originality in their genius than the modern ones have. They seem to me to have had more interesting shots of their own particular patent brands. There was that pitching shot with a straight-faced club of Mr. Ball's for one, and there was one of a different kind of Mr. Horace Hutchinson's. Who but that eminent genius would have dared to hold the mashie so loosely that the club "flopped" from the fingers into the web at the base of the thumb in the middle of the shot? Many people did that in driving but no on else in a short pitch. It was an audacious, almost impudent shot, but it did cut the legs from under the ball quite amazingly.

Today everything seems to have gotten more stereotyped and there is one bang with a driver and another bang with a mashie niblick and that is all.

The Half Scraper

I have lately picked up on a bookstall a quaint little book of games of just a hundred years ago. Therein, sandwiched between a treatise on game cocks and a mysterious pastime called "Eo," I found an account of "The Game of Golf," a favorite summer amusement in Scotland. Much of it was commonplace but the list of clubs I found very engaging. "There are six sorts of clubs," says the writer, "used by good players; namely the common club, used when the ball lies on the ground, the scraper and half scraper, when in long grass; the spoon, when in a hollow; the heavy iron club, when it lies deep among stones or mud; the light iron ditto, when on the surface of shingle or sandy ground."

The name that particularly took my fancy is that of the "half scraper." It is one I had never before heard but now on looking back, I think I must once have seen it employed. It must have been nearly twenty years ago on a most bitterly cold day by the sea that three of us set out to play a round. One whom I will call D found his ball lying ensconced in the neatest possible little rabbit scrape in the side of a knoll just beyond the first green. It appeared to us clearly unplayable but D declared that he had left behind in the clubhouse the one club that could deal with it.

We waited shivering in that wintry wind till the caddie returned bearing some form of niblick. D carefully inserted the head of the club into the rabbit scrape behind the ball and gave a vigorous tug at it. Out came the ball. It ran on and on and finished in the hole. I think it was greatly to our credit that we did not say a word about the rule concerning the ball being "pushed, scraped or spooned" nor did we as much as smile for three holes. Then we exploded into a burst of Homeric laughter and I do not believe that D knows why we laughed to this day.

That club of his was surely the half or indeed the whole scraper. We have been needing it badly of late on some of our inland courses as well as the "heavy iron club when it lies deep among mud." Snow followed by unresting rain has made a sad quagmire of many a pleasant park and I played on one the other day where my shoes were nearly pulled off my feet. Golf in such weather is not a good game and yet I daresay it is now and then good for us. It rubbed into me at any rate two familiar lessons that can never be too thoroughly learned.

There is nothing like rich, glutinous mud to make one lift one's head prematurely. One is frightened of a blob of mud in one's eye and also of getting the club stuck in the ground so that it will never come out again, after the manner of an unskillful oarsmen "catching a crab." The effort that is needed to keep that head resolutely down is really a heroic one. The second lesson was our old friend "Be up." One felt as if one was bewitched, so regularly did the ball stop short. I believe that in such conditions, there is only one thing to do. It is to determine to pitch—not run, for there is no run—past the hole. It is astonishing how seldom one does it even under the best conditions, but when one does, one wins the hole.

A Course
Without a Hole

I once wrote some account of a golf course that had only one hole, and one is generally deemed an irreducible minimum, but, in fact, by far the most exciting and nerve-racking course of my acquaintance possesses no holes at all. There is nothing to show that it is a golf course.

Scattered about the lawn and on the grass along the edges of the drive are a number of little white sticks, a net, a garden seat or two, and a derelict golf umbrella, being close to the front door and likely to make an unfavorable impression on callers, is objected to and sometimes even removed by the hostess, but it is always immediately and firmly replaced by the host. There is no putting—only pitching from the tee with a mashie niblick (7 iron), and the player whose ball lies nearest to the little white stick wins the hole.

At nearly every hole the player has only a tiny oasis of smooth grass round the stick to aim at, and he must fairly pitch on it and stop on it. Any ball that does not carry the intervening hazard—be it bench or umbrella, gravel walk or rough grass—is out of bounds; so is the ball that runs over into any of these unpleasantnesses. There is no running through bunkers, no winning a hole by having the better of two bad shots, no playing for the pusillanimous safety. If both players are out of bounds the hole is halved. You must either be on the green or you might as well be a hundred miles off.

It is the fiercest possible kind of golfing discipline, because you must "go out for the shot" every time, and every shot is so difficult that you are certain sooner or later to grow cramped with sheer terror. Now, if there is one stroke in the world in which freedom of striking is essential it is a mashie niblick shot played "to cut the legs from under the ball." You must take the club well back, you must hit the ball hard, and how can you do that when your nose is getting closer and closer to the ground and your paralyzed wrists refuse their office?

I suppose it is partly the nature of this particular shot that causes a particular psychological phenomenon to be so often observable on this course. Nowhere else in the world can you see such sudden and astonishing reversals of fortune. Once the holes begin to slip they slide like an avalanche. I have encountered and watched many very good players on the course, and they are none of them immune from the bacillus of collapse.

Only the other day I watched a young lady, whose pitching and placidity are equally famous. She was six up with seven to go, and playing, if I may so express it, like a diabolic angel, but she was pulled down with a rush to all square and one to play. The horrible feeling of the holes dropping away is accentuated a hundredfold because there are no halves for you to play for. Once the enemy is on the green you have got to be "inside him" or you are beaten. It may be imagined how overwhelming is the relief when he puts his tee shot out of bounds and you know that the rot is stopped for at least one hole.

The possibility of collapse and the difficulty of following the other fellow's shot are so well recognized that to give your opponent the honor on the first tee is deemed equal to giving him a perceptible start. If he gets into his stride with his first shot you may never catch him. So much so is this the case that the language of billiards is used on the course, and you may constantly hear, "Oh, yes—I was three up, but then he began a big break and it was all up." And it is wonderful what brilliant breaks even the most futile can occasionally make. The tee shots following one another so quickly, and there being no other shots in between, you get the touch of the green to perfection and may reel off half a dozen tee shots running that have all the rapidity and nicety of a professional playing nursery cannons.

As to the other man, although, of course, he tries to play too, he might, to all intents and purposes, just as well be the billiards challenger, sitting and glaring with stony indifference at the champion at the table. Then comes the turn of the tide. Your next tee shot, a miracle of boldness and backspin, falls on the gravel walk, short by a demi-semi fraction of an inch. The enemy takes his chance and gets in. Instantly the position is reversed. You are the challenger and he is dashing from tee to tee and planting shot after shot within inches of the stick. Down to four, down to three—two—one—all square—one down—oh, why were you ever born!

A Triumph of Courage

One fact stands out about Walter Hagen's victory at Hoylake. It is no disparagement of his skill to say that this was preeminently a victory of courage. Two or three people who were not at Hoylake said to me when I returned to London, in the identical words, "He must be the bravest golfer in the world." And I agreed with them.

I have seen Hagen himself play more convincing golf. I have certainly seen several other people play both more blamelessly and more brilliantly. But, as an example of sheer dogged sticking power, that long stern chase over the last nine holes, when he knew exactly what he had to do, and that a slip at any moment might prove fatal, was the finest thing of its kind I have ever seen, or ever hope to see.

For Hagen this whole championship was a long spell of being "up against it." His first qualifying round of 83, very, very nearly put him out of the running. He had to do a 73 at Formby to save his neck, and in that 73 most of the real life-saving work had to be done on the last nine holes. Then he began the championship with a 77, which though very far from bad, threw him some little way behind the leaders. His next two rounds of 73 and 74 put him at the top of the list equal with E. R. Whitcombe, and everybody thought he could win.

I came out to watch Hagen in his last round, when he had just completed the first nine holes in 41 with three sixes on his card. At the same moment came the news that Whitcombe, who had taken 43 for his first nine of this last round, had rallied in a brilliant manner to play the second nine in the superb total of 35, giving him a 78. Hagen then had 36 for the last nine to win and 37 to tie. Now I suppose that the strictest computation would make par for those last nine holes 34—4 3 4 3 4 4 4 4 4; but there are pars and pars. Three at least of the last five holes measure a good deal nearer 500 than 400 yards, and of the shorter ones, several possess in a cross wind almost infinite capacity for disaster.

The general opinion was that Hagen just could not reasonably do it. If he did not start home with four perfect holes, he had no chance, and even if he did, 5's were bound to creep in toward the finish. In fact he did not start home with four perfect holes, but he dropped only one stroke, getting a 4 at the eleventh instead of the par 3. But the wonderful thing was that he did not drop four strokes.

At each of the four holes he made a mistake, and two of them were bad mistakes, and yet he recovered! He holed a twenty-foot putt at the tenth, after taking three shots to reach the green. He laid a pitch out of difficult broken country dead at the twelfth, and at the thirteenth to get his 3 chipped to within five feet of the cup out of a bunker at the side of the green, which had caught his tee shot.

At this point, I think we who naturally wanted England to win, gave up hope. We began to feel that this was no man of flesh and blood, but some invulnerable demon who fate could not touch. And indeed he had performed such prodigies of recovery that one could not go on wishing him not to win. It would have been a positive shame, if any calamity had befallen him. In fact from this point on to the end, he never looked like making a mistake.

He did in stern fact make one slip. He hit two great wooden club shots to the edge of the sixteenth or "Dun" green, and then was short with his run-up, missed his putt and took a 5 for the hole, where a better approach might easily have given him a 4. But as results proved this was immaterial.

By common consent, his greatest shot was his second to the seventeenth, where there is a very narrow green cooped in between deep bunkers on the left and an out-of-bounds road at the right. The shot he had to play was one of 160 to 170 yards I suppose. It was in a sense no more than an ordinary firm iron shot and the ball lay well; a shot that all of us might be able to play, if it did not really matter. But in the circumstances, Hagen's shot—he laid it about ten feet from the hole—was one of the finest I ever saw, and this is a verdict to which I know his fellow professionals agreed. True he holed a good putt for his 4 on the home green, but it was this brave seventeenth that did it.

I could not help wondering while watching golf history thus unroll itself, whether one could have told from Hagen's demeanor the issue at stake. He took a great deal of trouble, but then he always does; he went for his long shots with any amount of dash, but he always does that too; he looked serene, but he never looks depressed. If he either smiled or spoke I did not notice it. I would not have undertaken to say whether he was leading the field by strokes, or hopelessly out of it, or as was the case in fact, at the crisis of his fate.

A Golfing Inferno

There is a story of a golfer who died and went down to the underworld of fire and brimstone. When he got there things did not appear to be as bad as he had been led to expect. In particular there stretched away in front of him apparently the most perfect golf course he had ever seen. Fairways, greens, all seemed ideal and he suggested to one of the other souls in pain that they should have a game.

"There are no balls," replied the other, "that's the hell of it."

When I read that pleasant little story (it may not be new to some of you, but it was new to me) it occurred to me to people in my imagination that nether-most hell of the golfer. Who are those that have not fully earned their places on that links of torment, by doing in life the greatest amount of harm to their fellow golfers? It seems to me that they are people whose names I do not even know. All trace of them has long since vanished from the earth, but the evil that they did lives after them, for they sowed a seed that was to germinate in the minds of generations of golfers yet unborn.

The first I should choose would be that unknown artist, who years ago, in the pages of ancient manuals, now to be found only amid collectors' treasures, drew the first picture of a golfer with his right elbow high in the air. For how much overswinging and slicing has that wretch been responsible! I have a perennial grievance against him. He is the man I want to get at. I like to think of him standing on the tee of the finest short hole in the world—some hole to which the fourth hole at the National Links or the third at Pine Valley is not even comparable in magnificence—with the most perfectly balanced of all irons in his hand, gnashing his teeth impotently because he has no ball with which to play the shot.

Some of the harm he did is dying out. Photography has superseded his art, and photography has shown that in fact the right elbow of good players is kept low and well in to the side. But for myself, a player of almost the prephotographic era, with an incorrigible elbow, I cannot quite find it in my heart to forgive him.

Standing beside him on that tantalizing tee I imagine the infamous villain, who described putting as an inspiration. It may be that he only dashed off the words thoughtlessly and light-heartedly, thinking that he had perpetrated a rather pretty epigram. But a man must be taken to intend the consequence of his acts, and there have been terrible consequences of these words.

Think of the hundreds of golfers, who when they were young and flexible might have been drilled or have drilled themselves into some reasonably sound and steady method of putting. Instead they believed it to be all a matter of chance and contented themselves with buying a new putter now and then, and hoping for the best. And now they have grown old in vice and it is too late to reform. There is just this to be said, that since they believe bad putting not to be their own fault, but the work of some malignant demon, they have not sorrowed over it too much. That may some day be accounted toward forgiveness for the maker of that fatal epigram.

Another denizen of my inferno must be the man who declared that on the full swing all the weight must on the way up be transferred from the left foot to the right. Just think of all the swaying and overbalancing, the ponderous heaving blows that he has caused! I am willing to believe that he meant well, as do many of the persons who do most damage in the world. He spoke something of a half truth, but he had much better have kept silent. How many right knees have crumpled and bent; how many left toes have pirouetted all too freely, because he did not! In his corner of the infernal regions there should always be a slicy wind blowing down the back of his neck.

Last comes he who christened the "wrist shot" and with him I think must go all those who have talked or written about wrists. Who can first hear of a wrist shot without visualizing a kind of scoop or flick with loose wrists bending at the joints? And was there ever a picture so ludicrously unlike the real thing? When we see a good golfer play a wrist shot, it is surely the firmness of his wrists that impresses us more than anything else.

I could add others to my ideal golfing hell as who of us could not, but I think I will stop at four. In this way I can mete out to them an even greater punishment. They will have a perfect course to play on and a perfect group as well—what a diabolical foursome—and yet no ball. How that will pay them back for their misdeeds! I must stop here or I will begin to feel sorry for them.

Self-Deception and Flattery

There are two distinct methods by which golfers endeavor to bring themselves to the best frame of mind in which to play the best golf that is in them. One is of an obvious nature, suited to simple, strong men. It consists in playing a series of hard matches against the fiercest available opponents. It is a strenuous treatment, with a flavor of kill or cure, and does not commend itself to those subtler and more "temperamental" persons, the bubble of whose vanity is easily pricked.

For these a course of deliberate self-deception and flattery is to be prescribed. They should choose someone whom they can outdrive and outplay: give him strokes, in order to save their self-respect, but not quite enough of them, in order to make tolerably sure of winning. They will soon find their confidence growing wonderfully.

I have to confess myself of this second class. I have always remembered a remark made to me by a shrewd, not to say cynical, friend some twenty-five years ago. I had been playing very badly in good company and my lamentations were doubtless excessively tiresome. "Never mind," said my friend, "go to your home course where you're cock of the walk, and then you'll soon get on your game again." With a mixture of shame and pleasure, I found his words come true. This flattering treatment can be overdone. It is apt to become enervating; but a judicious indulgence in it is most effective.

A short time ago I experienced a one-day's course of it and, as a result, am in a state of almost bloated conceit. It must be admitted that I have some cause, for I have found a golfer—"a being erect upon two legs and bearing the outward semblance of a man, and not a monster"—to whom I can give two strokes a hole. To be precise, it was one stroke at the three short holes and two at all the rest. We had two excellent matches, and I won one at the seventeenth, the other at the last hole. What could be better?

Moreover, I must make it clear that my opponent had played before—several times. Not merely that, but he had had lessons and acquired a driving style both of power and promise. I must not do myself the injustice of underrating his game. When he really hit the ball from the tee, he hit it rather farther than I could. Indeed as regards the long game, he almost hurt my vanity. At one hole, when he had surpassed my very best shot by a yard or two, he remarked, "I suppose if one took up this game and got any good at it, one would drive a good bit farther than that."

At that moment I began to doubt if I had after all, chosen quite the right medium for my treatment; but, if he made me feel a short driver, he also made me feel an uncannily accurate one. We were playing on a course which was, admittedly, ill-suited to a beginner. The rough was never far away and it was in its full midsummer luxuriance. So prodigal was he of his ammunition that at one time a shell shortage was seriously threatened. After the first four holes we calculated that the half-dozen "repaints" which he had bought would not hold out beyond the tenth. Fortunately the rate of consumption decreased, and I was not forced, as I had feared, to make him an advance from my own stock.

He played one or two holes quite magnificently. Are there not many middle-aged gentlemen, with handicaps of no more than 10 or 12, who would give their eyes to reach the eighth hole at Woking with a drive and a flick with a mashie. That is what my opponent did, and very nearly holed his putt for 3. And yet I beat him!

Truth will out, and his short game was weak. If I had played another day's golf with him I should have come to fancy it a more remarkable feat than it really is to get nearer to the hole with an approach putt than the place you start from. I had expected him to putt well. I recollected a teacher of mathematics who declared that he found his knowledge of planes and angles of great use to him on the green. Now my opponent was a full-blown professor, and a young one, and so I was prepared for anything; but I can only suppose that his are not quite the right sort of mathematics for the purpose.

There was one thing about the game which rather wounded me. We had a gallery of three, whom we had brought over expressly to lunch and watch us play. They walked all the way round and were much interested, but their interest centered entirely round my opponent. I might "shoot birdies" by flocks, and, the tees being pleasantly short, I did in fact shoot two or three, but I could attract no attention to myself whatever.

"That was a three," I would say reproachfully, and they would only reply "Oh." *His* shots, on the other hand, were received with partisan war-whoops of joy. I felt that I was emphatically not the idol of the crowd. And yet I was not ungenerous. A lady of my acquaintance always allows herself three "cheats" in a game of Patience. Well, I allowed him at least three cheats, besides his strokes, and still there appeared to be an impression that I was "unsportsmanlike."

However, they were only poor, ignorant creatures. Possibly they were so ignorant that they expected me to do 3's. I think that must have been the reason. Now that I have hit on that, the slight chill which I felt has turned into a genial glow. As I have not played since, the treatment is at present perfectly successful.

How to Get Your Game Back

In fairy stories, the hero is often given by a good fairy or sometimes by a bad, deceitful magician, the power of wishing for anything he likes. As many as three wishes are occasionally granted him, though when this is done by the bad magician there is invariably a catch in it. The nearest approach to it, in my experience, was the advertisement of a magician in a London newspaper who declared he could teach long driving and perfect putting in a single lesson for a fee of a guinea. I did not pay my guinea and cannot help suspecting that there was a catch in it somewhere.

I have sometimes amused myself by thinking what my wishes would be, should a beneficent fairy ever come along, and I believe I know one of the mental gifts to ask her for. It is the power of knowing when to begin thinking and when to stop thinking. That is, I admit, a cryptic sentence: so let me explain. It is clear that no sane golfer, after making one indifferent shot, should instantly begin to puzzle his head as to why he made it. It is equally clear that after weeks of bad shots, he must perceive that there is something wrong and set his brain to work to find out what it is. The difficulty is at exactly what point he should begin; how many bad shots justify self examination?

Now for the other side of the question. When he has at length hit a good shot again, he must not instantly forget the why and the wherefore and abandon himself to delirious slogging. Yet if he continues to think too long, to admire and imitate his own virtues, to remember religiously the particular remedy that cured him last Tuesday week, he will grow cramped and artificial and sooner or later will have a bad breakdown. As before, it is a question of the magical, the psychological moment. Exactly when should he forget the cure and remember only, with due gratitude to Heaven, that he is on his game?

"There is one illustrious and venerable sage," wrote the author of "The Art of Golf," "of whom it is proverbial that not even a whole round of bad shots will tempt him to consider his position. 'I've missed the ball' is all he says. To hit it again is all he tries." That is a difficult standard to live up to. There are few golfers, of so Spartan a habit and so blank a mind, as not to think about their wrists or legs or elbows in the course of so wholly disastrous a round.

Yet I believe most of us would be restored to golfing health all the more quickly if we could make for ourselves a self-denying ordinance, and refrain from thinking for this minimum of one whole round.

Suppose we are out of practice and have not played for a long time, it is only natural that we should feel a little stiff and ungainly, that our eye should be out. Obviously we ought to give Nature a chance before we begin, metaphorically, to take drugs. I remember that when I came home after the war and went away for a first holiday to a seaside golf course, I made a solemn vow, that I would just try to hit the ball stolidly and stupidly and think of nothing else for two days. I played at least respectably.

It is a different and more difficult matter when we are in full practice and have been playing well. Then the first lapse comes with a horrid shock of surprise. We imagined that we could not do such a thing. The temptation to put things right again by a little experiment is almost overpowering. Yet I am disposed to think that it is just at this moment that we ought to make the mind a blank. Our golfing health has been so robust that this germ of disease cannot have had time to make serious inroads. If we disregard it, it will very probably expire quickly of inanition. If we feed it on our unsuccessful theories, it will grow fat and flourishing and hard to be rid of. My metaphors may be a little mixed and I admit I cannot follow my own advice, but I believe it to be sound.

67

As regards the precious moment at which to forget and lash out, I may quote another remark of that wisest of philosophers, Sir Walter Simpson. "Golf," he says, "refuses to be preserved like dead meat in tins. It is living, human and free, ready to fly away at the least sign of an attempt to catch and cage it."

What a good phrase that is and what sturdy common sense likewise! And yet it would be rash to say that we should never pigeon-hole our painfully acquired knowledge against future breakdowns. I believe we ought to try temporarily to forget on a progressive system. For our first few drives, after the wonderful driving cure has been found, we should remember it every time. Then we should gently remind ourselves of it only on every third tee, then on every sixth and so on in a diminishing scale. Of course that is not advice to be taken literally, but we ought gradually to think less and less till at last all that remains is a mental picture, which does not need actively recalling of ourselves doing the right thing, not the wrong.

One of the dangers of thinking too hard and too long about a particular system is that we come to depend on it too completely and when, as is inevitable, we miss, we accept this as evidence of the failure of the system. It does not occur to us that it may have happened because we violated some elementary principle. Mr. Grantland Rice, I think, pointed this out in an excellent article on "No Fool-Proof Tips." It is not the fault of the system that we swing too fast or take our eye off of the ball. And after all, we must miss occasionally for no definite reason except that we are human.

When we are playing well and confidently, we accept an occasional miss as proceeding from that cause and think no more of it. But when we are just recovering from a bad spell, we are exceedingly illogical. Instead of being humbly grateful that we are at least hitting some shots: instead of hoping that we shall gradually come to hit more, we hail the first bad shot as if it were the end of the world. Not to be such a fool—that is another wish I must remember when the good fairy arrives.

The Passing of Ben Sayers

The death of Ben Sayers removes from the world of golf a notable figure; one that can never be replaced, and one that deserves something more than the "passing tribute of a sigh."

Ben was a great little golfer: it was truly amazing what he accomplished with only his five feet, three or four inches to help him. He was a link, one of the very few remaining ones, between the past and the present. In his first tournament, David Strath had led the field and Strath had been the great rival of the famous "young Tommy" Morris who died almost in the plenitude of his powers far away back in the 1870s. Yet Ben lived to fight and hold his own with the Vardons, Braids and Taylors, yes, and the Duncans and Rays. More than everything else, Ben was a "character," a creature of infinite humor, a personality round which legends clustered thickly, such as is more and more rarely to be found among the smart, trim, orthodox, knicker-bockered professionals of today.

In one respect Ben always seemed to me a little misunderstood. People thought of him always as a cunning little man. So in a sense he was cunning. He understood the weaknesses of his brother golfers. No one had a keener eye for what may be called "stunts" that should appeal to them and draw money from their pockets. He could always invent a club to sell to them with an alluring name. Such was his pitcher called the "Benny." Such was his "Dreadnought" driver with its big head and long shaft with the spring "under the hands" which ravaged the whole country about 1900 or 1910—the most successful of all his devices.

But it was not only Ben's commercial shrewdness that made him a skillful salesman. Combined with it he had a perennially boyish enthusiasm. When he invented a club, he really believed, and not merely said, that it was the club of all the

69

ages. He was forever thinking that he had discovered some new way of swinging the club or playing a particular shot that was to beat the world. His nephew, Jack White, another admirable and successful club-maker, has inherited I think something of this delightful keenness, this ever-fresh hopefulness, and it was this quality quite as much as or more than his shrewdness that made the success of Ben Sayers.

I feel tempted to make a comparison from another walk of life. People used to say of Lord Northcliffe, the newspaper magnate, that his success was due to his knowing exactly what interested the man on the street. I am not sure that his real secret was not rather that he took an interest in so many things and by his genius for enthusiasm made the man in the street interested too.

It was this wonderful vitality and keenness that made of Ben Sayers a really fine golfer when he was over sixty and his less hopeful contemporaries had thought it time to retire. He would not acknowledge, even to himself, that he was old or that the young men were too strong. I remember well the meeting of Gleneagels in 1919. The course was then prodigiously long—the carries made J. H. Taylor mop his brow—and all the cream of the professional ranks was there. Ben had I think hurt himself; at any rate by some mischance he could not play and he could not have been more disappointed if he had been a young apprentice longing to win his spurs. "And me playin' so awfu' weel jist now" he exclaimed in tones of tragic regret. He saw himself in his mind's eye beating all the champions at the age of 62 and I have no manner of doubt he would have made a bold show of it.

Though he never won the Championship, Ben was undoubtedly a good golfer. He was believed to have tied for it with Jack Burns and, I think, David Anderson at St. Andrews in 1888 and then, on the cards being checked, it was discovered that Burns had won by a stroke. "Give me a wind and I'll show you who'll be Champion" was one of his famous utterances before a Championship at Muirfield, a course he knew in and out, but he never could quite do it.

At North Berwick in the 1880s, when the course was very short, his fame was monumental. With his skill in pitching and running and putting and his knowledge of the tricky little rules, he was as near as might be invincible and when he was rather older and the course a good deal longer, he held almost the same unchallenged sovereignty. "Beaten by 6 and 5 on my own course. It's no possible but it's a fact," he said, after the late F. G. Tait had played an irresistible round against him, and it was no unfair statement of his position at North Berwick. Though his chief strength lay in his short game, he was yet no mean driver; with a very long club, which seemed to waggle him like the proverbial tail that wags the dog, he could hit both far and sure, and he was a sterling match player who could in his own words "always come up to time when the bell rang."

Probably Ben's most historic match was that in 1901 when he and his brother-in-law, David Grant, played Hugh and Andrew Kirkaldy a home and home foursome over North Berwick and St. Andrews. The brothers were in the height of their power and the two little men from North Berwick were thought to have been over-ambitious, but Grant said to Ben, "There's not much between any men, who can play at all, when once the money's on." In fact the North Berwick couple won so many holes over their own course as to demoralize their foe and they ended the whole match 12 up with 11 to play.

Ben also had another great home and home match—a single— against Andrew Kirkaldy. He gained six holes at North Berwick, but Andrew's first round at St. Andrews was such a fine one that the six holes were reduced to a single one. In the afternoon that one disappeared also, and the match was square with five to go. Then Sayers did those last five in twenty strokes, tremendous golf with a gutty ball, and won the match by two holes. I think it was on that occasion that "Big Crawford" the celebrated caddie proposed to kiss Ben and no doubt the little man owed much in these matches to the big one. Crawford was a formidable body guard to have on one's side.

"And that's the Referee" he once menacingly remarked, producing a vast fist, when his interpretation of the rules was not acceptable.

Ben and Andrew Kirkaldy were great in combination as well as in enmity and there are many old stories about them. Andrew has told one of them in his book. Ben put their ball on the railway in a big foursome at St. Andrew's and it lay near a sleeper among some stones. Said Andrew, "Ye ken that short-headed wee mashie of yours. Could you let me have it to play the shot?" "Na, na, Andrew," said Ben. "Ye're only wantin' my club for fear of breaking your ain. Play awa' and dinna be feart."

Another classic story of Ben is that he disappeared into a big bunker and seemed to take a long time over the shot, whereupon someone asked what he was doing. "You may be sure he's no wastin' his time," was the reply. There is about it a touch of unkindness. Times have changed and Ben belonged to a generation which held perhaps slightly different views from ours as to what is legitimate in the way of winning a match. But none of his maneuvers could ever raise anything but a smile. He was a most disarming little man and he will always be pleasantly as well as freshly remembered.

Eighteen Down with
None to Go

In one respect the golfer of today is a softer and more pampered creature than he of yesterday. When he plays in a team match, he knows that the most he can lose for his side is a single point. If he is beaten by the greatest of all margins it is true that his disgrace may be blazoned abroad in the shape of a horrid little "10 and 8" inside a bracket, but he cannot bring his whole side crashing down with him—his liability is limited to that one point.

It was not ever thus, and until the early years of the present century the scores in team matches were reckoned by the more manly, more brutal, if you will, method of holes. There used to be an old gentleman at St. Andrews, General Briggs by name, one of whose sayings was often quoted: "When I am five up I strive to be six up: when I am seven up I strive to be eight up." That was the spirit in which team matches were played in the consulship of Planeus. There was no stopping after you had the match won. You went on winning as many holes or losing as few as you could to the bitter end.

There used to be tragedies, but it was good discipline. And there were compensations in defeat. Sometimes the man who lost most was frantically acclaimed because he had just contrived not to lose too many. There was once a match in Yorkshire in which all the couples had finished save one. Side A was ten up but the last man on side B was nine down and three holes left to play. Everyone came out to watch him: amid breathless excitement he halved all three. His side won by a hole and he was carried with wild cheers into the clubhouse, the hero of the day who had only lost nine holes out of eighteen.

That is the bright side of the picture. Now for a story of the gloomy side. The Oxford and Cambridge match of 1908—over thirty-six holes—was played at Hoylake. Cambridge won by twenty-three holes to twenty-two and this is how it happened. The Oxford captain had had a terrible time of it and lost his match by 10 and 8. But, of course, he couldn't retire to the clubhouse, find a dark corner to sit down in and order a beer. He had to continue to play the remaining eight holes of the round. He lost the first two of those eight and that made twelve down. He spurted, got back the next two and so was only ten down.

Then arrived the news that, with only this one match to finish, Oxford led by twelve. Promptly the poor Oxford captain lost three more holes in row. He halved the last but a half was not enough. Oxford had lost the match by a single hole and their own captain had contributed thirteen holes towards their defeat. It was altogether too harrowing: even Cambridge stood silent, too sorry for the victim to acclaim their own hero, and after that the match has always been reckoned by the more merciful method.

All sorts of ingenious reasons were advanced for the change. It was said that the winning or losing of the match was the only thing that counted in golf: that if the reckoning were by holes every member of a side ought to know exactly how every other member of it stood at any particular moment, in order that he should steer his course accordingly. But this is all casuistry of the most patent kind. The real reason for the change was sheer tenderness of heart towards other unfortunates who might in the future be thirteen down.

The worst tragedy of my own I can recall was an eleven down—in thirty-six holes—and the greatest triumph a fourteen up, in eighteen, but certainly my most agonizing moment came in my first year at Cambridge when I went to play on the historic course on Blackheath. There were but seven holes and we had to play them three times and at the end of the first round, I—poor frightened freshman—occupying the post of honor against the leading Manchester player—was seven down. There seemed at the moment no earthly reason why I should not be twenty-one down and I can still remember with what joyful surprise I halved the eighth hole. It seemed almost too good to be true that I could not lose in all more than twenty holes. I think my adversary must have deliberately relented for in the end I was but five down. At the time I plumed myself a little on my supposed powers of recovery but I am older now, and can be grateful to my enemy for his kindness. He would deny it, I know, but I think he did it on purpose.

Even if I had been twenty down on that dreadful day, I should not have been a world's record holder because there was once a gentleman who achieved finality in this matter by being eighteen holes down on an eighteen-hole course. He afterwards wrote to the papers—unwisely as I think—to explain that he had had influenza and was playing with a borrowed pack of clubs. His explanation rather than his actual achievement has made him immortal.

1925

Take Your Fun Seriously

I had almost given up all hope of reading a new book on golf, or rather, to be precise, a new kind of golf book. Another and another and another, I know for my sins, I shall have to read, and every one of them will begin with the length and weight of the author's clubs and a minute description of the overlapping grip. Have I not had a hand in writing some such books myself, and do I not know better than anyone their tediousness? Am I not still so childish as to read them in the hopes of finding some tip that was meant expressly for my private salvation? But a new kind of book about golf? Of that I had despaired and now lo! I have found it.

This book is called "J. H. Taylor or the Inside of a Week," and it is by Mr. Harold Begbie, a well known writer here on a variety of other subjects, who has hitherto been guiltless of a golf book. It is not only a new sort of book but an odd sort of book. The illustrious Taylor is a great reader, and the favorite among all his books is Boswell's "Life of Johnson." It is only right and proper then that he should have a Boswell of his own, and Mr. Begbie has played the part.

These two went away together for "the inside of a week." They stayed somewhere in an old-fashioned inn close to a golf course on a country common. Where it is they do not reveal, but it sounds charmingly rustic and unsophisticated with gorse and heather, geese, ducks and the village pond as the chief hazards and occasionally an impious horseman galloping over the putting green. Everyday they played golf and in the evening they talked. They talked a great deal in the intervals of "J. H." leaping to his feet to demonstrate the action of the left wrist by making the poker whistle through the air, and Mr. Begbie has written down as much as he can remember of the tempestuous flood that came from the great man's lips. And he has done it very well.

Here is Taylor to the life, full of keenness about everything, now praising to the skies, now vehemently denouncing, now making the dust rise in clouds from the hotel carpet as he shows how a mashie shot should be played "firmly, sir, firmly!" (this with a formidable shake of this head, I am sure). There never was such a tremendous person as Taylor; he lives in superlatives; the sound and fury of his opinions are sometimes almost overpowering, but nobody could possibly help feeling respect and affection for him. He is not only a remarkable golfer but a remarkable man and a lovable man too.

If Taylor had not been a professional golfer, he would certainly have made his mark in some other walk of life, and I hazard the guess that he would have been a member of Parliament. At any rate he would have been riding on some crusade carrying some fiery cross for the benefit of his fellow men. When he was a boy at Westward Ho! carrying clubs and doing odd jobs, he was one of a large family with poor parents trying to do their best for their children. To his father and mother he pays a simple and touching tribute and those hard times in his youth have given him an abiding sympathy for those whose way in life is drab and hard. He wants them all to look after their internal economies and to play more games out of doors.

"Give the modern Englishman his playground," he exclaims, "and he will waste no time in listening to a tub-thumper's rehearsal of his economic wrongs and no money in feathering the nest of the political agitator. He'll save his money to buy the implements of his game, and he'll spend his time in practicing his game till he is perfect at it." And this theme is elaborated at some length. Taylor is truly in earnest about it and has done his bit by taking a big part in obtaining the public course in Richmond Park where so many Londoners now play that I am told it takes four hours to get round.

A little later we find Mr. Begbie tremblingly confessing to playing well one day and ill another and his master thunderously admonishing him. "Weakened character," says Dr. Johnson—I mean Dr. Taylor—"is a shameful thing and weakness of character alone can account for such variability as you have the shocking brazenness to describe. But see how beautifully golf may help and strengthen a man's moral character. Suppose a miserable long-handicap man came to the reasonable conclusion that his contemptible unsteadiness is the consequence of a feeble and sickly will; by dint of improving his golf he must at the same time improve his moral life."

Rather an alarming companion for a golfing weekend, this Dr. Taylor. But he is less ogreish than he appears. He wants to help us as long as we strive to do our best. The only person he despises is the man who does not try to play golf as well as he can, who does not "take his fun seriously."

Coming Back
Fresh To It

When this article appears September will have flown. It will be idle to deny that autumn is on us. Some enthusiastic American golfers will, I suppose, be beginning to bemoan the fact that the end of the golfing season is in sight, that within a certain number of weeks treasured clubs must be put away and retire, like our old friend Caesar, into winter quarters. They may perhaps be inclined to envy their British brethren who, save for an occasional day of frost or a flurry of snow, may hope to play their game the whole year round.

Doubtless a long period of abstinence is hard to endure, and yet there is something to be said for it. To the players of other games a rest is considered almost essential. If, for instance, a cricketer after a season in England goes on an Australian tour through the winter months and then has to face another summer of play at home, he is deemed to have every excuse if his game lacks its old sting.

Why should not the golfer also be the better for a rest and a good long one? Moreover, it is not only a question of playing well but of playing with enjoyment. I remember very well in 1913 having a round at Glenview with that excellent golfer, Mr. Ned Sawyer, and his telling me how at the beginning of a new season he was positively in a fever till he had broken 80. That is an enviable state of mind, to come back to a noble dish with so fresh and unjaded a palate as to be able to taste its flavor to the utmost. These thoughts came into my head only a few days ago when I went down to one of the best beloved of our seaside courses, Rye, to play in a friendly match against the Harlequins. The Harlequins are Oxford cricketers of distinction, and in the middle of a tour of cricket matches they take one day every summer to exchange their bats for clubs and play this golf match. Neither they, nor we their opponents, had played more than a round or so during the hot

81

weeks of June and July, when amateur golf here takes a little siesta. And I never saw any set of golfers more palpably enjoy the game for its own sweet sake. Neither, although this was not the main point, did we play particularly ill.

There were perhaps more elementary errors, more tee shots hit bang on the top, more pitches fluffed into cross bunkers at the player's toes. The out-of-practice eye, when it does come off the ball, does so in no uncertain manner. Yet on the whole the golf was as good as we had any right to expect and one or two rounds were quite sparkling.

At such a moment we really appreciate the sensuous pleasure of hitting a golf ball. For the case of a few lucky golfers familiarity with the full drive off the middle of the club may at times breed a certain measure of contempt. But when they come back to it after a rest they realize what a beautiful thing it is. They are like the man who smokes his first cigarette after smarting for some weeks in the fires of abstinence. That cigarette, and even one or two of its immediate successors, are like no others in the world. It is so good that I have sometimes been tempted to wonder whether those virtuous persons who give up tobacco in Lent really do from selfish and self indulgent motives. At any rate, it is the same with these first shots at golf, we may even plunge into a bunker, niblick in hand, full of the joy of life.

There is also the satisfaction of feeling that our old crimes are things of the past, and that we are starting with a clean sheet. It is as if some healing downpour had washed our sodden brains clear of all manner of clogging "tips" and theories.

If, as is likely enough, our first shot is a slice or else a hook, we do not say to ourselves "There is that wretched right elbow again"; we just try to hit the ball the next time. I would not go so far as to say that our minds should be wholly blank, that we should merely revel in hitting. It is the time for thinking of the quite primitive and elemental things which we learned when the world was young—slow back, and the eye on the ball.

The eye that has not been looking at a golf ball for some while does want to leap up; the club does want to go back too swiftly out of pure exuberance of enjoying itself. Both need a little benignant, fatherly curbing from their owner. But as to the rest—all the tiresome elbows and knees and feet and wrists that we're sent with into the world to plague golfers—they can be left for a little while to look after themselves. If we miss a shot, well—we have missed it, and there is much virtue in Sir Walter Simpson's "Aim more carefully."

Those of us who played golf as small boys can still remember the exquisite thrill of coming back to the game in the holidays after the long summer term was over, on the same course where we had played the summer before. It was so wonderful to find that just because we had grown bigger and stronger the bunkers which used to catch our longest shots were now carried with ease. We do not grow stronger nowadays, and if we grow bigger it is only round the waist. We cannot recapture the old sensation but we can come nearer to doing so by giving golf a periodical rest than by any other means.

I have not played since I was at Rye and fortunately I shall not play for another week when I set off on the romantic night train for St. Andrews. But I am looking forward with a childish eagerness to topping my first tee shot there and for the moment I refuse to pity those of my American brethren who will put away their clubs when winter comes.

There is one golfing story which always fill me with awe. It is that of a hero of antiquity, Sir Robert Hay, who, being asked at the end of a round what his score had been, replied that there were only two days in the year on which he could answer such a question, the spring and autumn tournament medal days.

It is a story which makes one writhe with embarrassment and misery on the victim's behalf. It was such a devastating snub, administered, as we may be sure, with a stately and freezing courtesy. The name of the wretched being history does not record, though there may be, for all I know, a tradition of it jealously guarded among a few St. Andrews families.

I can only picture the poor fellow for myself. He seems to me, even before the catastrophe, to have worn something of a humble, even a cringing, air. He was acutely conscious of the glory of being seen to speak to Sir Robert in public; fate had sent him at last an opportunity, and he had long since carefully thought out this ingratiating question. Then came a blinding flash from Olympus, and he was a broken man ever afterwards.

It may be plausibly argued that that memorable rebuke has produced its effect a long time after it was spoken. Nothing will ever prevent us from reckoning up our score, if it be a good one, and misstating it by a stoke or two. But there are today fewer people than there were when golf was young who write their scores down on paper.

If we could live up to Sir Robert's views in their full purity, we should tell a notably smaller number of lies in the course of a year; we should never see the odious spectacle of one player holing out while the other has walked off the green; we should be, in the sense in which Sir Robert would have employed the words, better golfers; but it is, I am afraid, more than doubtful whether we should be better hitters of the golf ball.

However much we may sometimes be bored by the man who insists on counting his score, it is hard to deny that it does good to his game. The American golfer takes, as a rule, a passionate interest in his score and, which is more than his British brother often does, he counts it with remarkable scrupulousness. He does not, as we often do, make sure of a short putt by attacking it with one hand and counting it in if it goes in and equally in if it does not. His honesty and his enthusiasm alike forbid such a proceeding, and so at the end of a round he does, as nearly as may be, know his score.

The result may been seen in American golfing literature, where the different classes of golfers are described not, as in our case, by their handicaps, but in such phrases as "those who play around in the low eighties," or even "the hundred men." This last expression is a coruscating testimony to truthfulness, for I do not remember for many years to have heard anybody come into a British clubhouse and declare a score of three figures. Yet I think there must be some entitled to do so, because two amateur competitors reached the "coveted century" in the qualifying rounds of a recent open championship.

There is little doubt that some small part of the excellence of the American amateur is due to this constant striving after a low score. He never grows slack; he has always a stimulus and a standard; he does not grow self-satisfied through some cheap victory, because he always aims at a victory over himself.

I am not much in love with the keeping of scores, and am certainly not contemplating a crusade in its favor, but honesty compels the admission that it is very good discipline. If we all did it, I suppose many of us would have to confess something that we now studiously conceal from ourselves, the painful fact that we are not playing up to the label affixed to us by the handicapping committee. As it is, the revelation comes as a sudden shock.

A Tip Fiend

As I write I am awaiting with ill-suppressed impatience the next issue of *The American Golfer*. I am always glad to see it but I am particularly eager this time because it should contain the winning tip in the competition for "The Tip that Has Helped Me Most." As soon as I have torn open the wrapper I shall be hard at it trying that tip in my room and probably I shall sneak off to a golf course to try it—with a really live ball—in the afternoon.

It may be thought I am of an imperishably, nay absurdly youthful and sanguine nature, to hope that after forty years of golf, this latest of many thousand tips is going to turn me into a golfer at last. Not at all. I live in no such fool's paradise. I wish I did, for it would be a very happy place of residence. But the trying of tips has become an ingrained habit. I could not give it up if I wanted to. It would make a hideous gap in my life so that I should have in despair to turn to knitting for an occupation. To "try everything once" may not make for good golf but once a man has become a tip-fiend, it is the only thing that can give him ease.

It is really astonishing how much fun and how little bitterness can be extracted from tips, once we have in our inmost hearts resigned ourselves, as far as it can be done, to a certain definite status in golf. When we are very ambitious it is undeniably disappointing to find that a crook of the little finger is not in fact going to translate us into a new and higher realm. But, once we have become a little sadder and wiser, we can get an enormous amount of fun out of a new tip, without believing that it is one of the eternal verities. "Let us live for the day" we say to ourselves, which, being interpreted, means, "Anyhow this may put me on my driving for this afternoon which will enable me to beat Jones, which will be very good fun. As to the next day—well, perhaps I shall have thought of a new tip by that time."

Yet I must admit to one weakness. I have just enough child-ish faith in tips left to make me unwilling to impart my latest one to anyone else. If I were to do so, I feel that the virtue would straightway go out of it—or out of me. It is a despicable superstition, no doubt, but I cannot help it. When Jones says to me "You seem to be driving much better than usual today. What is your latest dodge?" I shall lie to him unblushingly, saying in an airy manner, "Yes—I do seem to be hitting them decently for once. Goodness knows why—perhaps because I am not thinking about it." And all the while—a most contempt-ible person that I am—I shall be whispering over and over again to myself the latest magic formula. The human golfer is in-deed a strange animal.

I do not wish to appear too cynical. I believe there is always hope in a tip for any of us. But in that case it is not generally a new one at all. It is rather a very old one dressed up in a new and seductive guise which makes a sudden appeal to us. Let us take the case of so many of us who are confirmed "snatchers" in the back swing. It is of no use for anyone to tell us or for us to tell ourselves at this time of day to go "Slow back." We do not react to that formula. The words have grown so familiar as practically to have lost their meaning.

Neither would it be of value, save to the few classically minded, to say instead "Festina lente." But if some ingenious teacher tells us, by way of example, to start the club back with the left hand he may make us do what he wants without our knowing it and as long as we do not discover that his tip is the old "slow-back" in another guise, it may do us all the good in the world.

On another day the very same sort of thing may befall us in regard to "Keep your eye on the ball." To be told that quite baldly would only bore us but suppose we are told to see the club hit the ball—the effect may be magical. We find it rather an "intriguing" game of hide and seek to watch out for that club at the moment of its striking the ball and we do strike it accordingly.

Or take again another old friend, "Follow through." That is far too simple a remedy for our disease. It is like bathing in the waters of the Jordan. But let some more Machiavellian person stick a row of matches in the ground beyond the ball and urge us to try to strike them with the clubhead. Straightway we shall take a childish pleasure in this game of fire-works and so shall follow through in spite of ourselves.

There are, of course, some tips—and useful ones, too—that can hardly be put into any terse or intelligible form of words. They consist rather in attaining to a certain state of feeling. One of the most valuable lessons ever given me came from the illustrious James Braid. He did it not by words but by demonstration and I know what he "looked like" when he demonstrated and what I ought to "feel like" if I obey his commands. But if I were to attempt to explain in writing I should fill several pages and be incomprehensible at the end of them.

Tips of that kind are strictly personal ones. They belong to ourselves, and we find them almost impossible to pass on.

As I meditate on that tip and on how I am going to put it once more into practice at my next weekend on a famous seaside course, I find my cynical mood passing. After all perhaps something wonderful is going to happen to me. I am more than ever anxious for my *American Golfer*. Hark! there is a loud rat-tat on the door. It may be, it must be, the postman's knock!

Youth and
Crabbed Age

As a rule I do not venture to intrude our more prosaic golfing affairs on American readers, but a contest between youth and age is of some interest to all golfers who must consider themselves either young or old, and last week at St. Andrews saw one, I think, which is worth mentioning.

It took place in the Jubilee vase which is our most important handicap tournament of the year. It attracts a large number of the best amateur golfers who belong to the Royal and Ancient and takes a very great deal of winning, especially by those handicapped at scratch or thereabouts. Youth was represented by Mr. Tolley and age by Mr. Spencer Gollan, who ultimately won the tournament. He is 67 or 68 years of age, and has had the misfortune to lose the sight of one eye; so that to play two rounds a day on a long course in a most boisterous and fatiguing wind was, whatever his handicap, a considerable physical effort.

But Mr. Gollan has been a great all-round athlete. He has been a boxer and a rider and a sculler. He has done all these things very well, and he is as strong as a horse and as hard as iron. When he was about thirty-nine he began to play golf and three months afterward he reached the final of the Calcutta Cup—the other handicap tournament at St. Andrews—and was just beaten. Two years later he returned to the assault and won it, but that was five and twenty years ago, when he was a promising young player of forty or a little more. Therefore the handicappers this year gave him fourteen, and in this tournament fourteen means fourteen; there is no giving three-quarters of the odds; the receiver gets his full number of strokes.

Now Mr. Gollan naturally cannot hit the ball as far as he once could but he can still hit it some way, and he taught everyone a lesson in the art of cutting his coat according to his cloth, standing still, hitting gently, and maneuvering for the best strategic position for the next shot. He might not be able to reach the long par-four holes in two strokes, but he could make certain with a deadly certainty of getting them in two and a bit, and holing out in two putts. Against this tempestuous wind going out at St. Andrews, where there is but one par 3 in the nine holes, he did a string of fives with now and again a four, and who was going to give fourteen strokes to that? In his first three or four rounds he was averaging 84 or 85, and Mr. Tolley, despite the fact that he was doing 74's and 75's, had humanly speaking, no chance on earth of giving Mr. Gollan seventeen strokes. That was what he had to do since he owned three strokes, and three and fourteen make seventeen. And yet he succeeded in doing it.

It was in some ways a most interesting, and some ways a disappointing match. Mr. Gollan fell away from his steadiness and Mr. Tolley from his brilliancy, and for sixteen holes were a little depressed rather than thrilled. At the end of them Mr. Gollan stood dormie two. He had of course a stroke at each of the last two holes, and the seventeenth at St. Andrews, well over four hundred yards long with its slippery little green perched between the devil of the bunker and the deep sea of the road, is an ideal one for the man who can afford to play safely for his five. That was Mr. Gollan's case and in four shots his ball was safely at the hole side and there was his five waiting for him.

Mr. Tolley had to do the most perilous hole in the world in a three to save his neck. He hit a vast drive over the sheds, played a bold run up and then ran down a seven-yard putt. Even so, all seemed over for the last hole is three hundred and sixty-four yards long with nothing in particular in the way. Another three was needed and even that would probably not be good enough. The wind was blowing right behind the players and Mr. Tolley clearly intended to drive the green or die in the attempt.

It is rather exciting to see a man deliberately framing to drive three hundred and sixty-four yards, and that with an up slope in front of the green. It is still more exciting to see him do it. The ball pitched as it seemed quite close to the green, went on into the deep hollow still full of running, scaled the slope, ran on again and finished some ten yards to the left of the hole. In the circumstances it was one of the most tremendous shots I ever saw. Small wonder that even Mr. Gollan, man of granite as he is, wilted a little. He was weak all the way and took five, and Mr. Tolley had achieved the impossible and halved the match. These two threes had redeemed everything.

Unfortunately the two did not meet again to play it off. In this tournament there is no going to the nineteenth hole; both players pass through into the next round and in this case the luck of the draw separated them. Mr. Tolley went down in the next round, being in a very erratic mood. Not so Mr. Gollan, who resumed his steady gait and was never seriously pressed again.

There was one little characteristic incident in one of his matches that I must relate. Going to the tenth hole Mr. Gollan was badly hit on the wrist by an errant ball from another match. He did not mention it to his adversary who had not seen it, licked the cut, played his shot and did the hole in a birdie three. It was only several hours afterwards that the adversary by chance heard of it. That is a fine piece of toughness whether a man is 68 or 18.

The Ball That Cannot Be Sliced

Every individual hair of my head stood on end when I read, a day or two ago, an article in our English *Golf Illustrated*. It declared that an "un-named man of science in the midlands had discovered a golf ball which, owing to a particular and nicely adjusted marking would spin neither to the right nor to the left and, however cut, flew straight in the direction in which it was hit." The death-ray, I thought, was nothing to this. Here was the end of golf and so, in effect, of the world. The statement that the experiment was a "wholly scientific" one did not console me. Some one man who had been chronically afflicted by a slice or a hook would take to the ball and everyone else would have to follow suit in self defence and the game would be ruined.

Then I read on a little further and found some comfort, for it was said that in addition to its other qualities the ball refused to soar; "its tendency was earthwards." If that be so, golf may yet be saved. The ball will only be a good ball at a hole where the fairway is very narrow, the ground very hard and full of running and there are no cross hazards. An effective spoke can be put in its wheel, if such a metaphor be permissible, by the building of good old-fashioned ramparts across the course. Yes, I think that ought to do it, that is indeed if the scientific gentleman in the midlands and his ball really exist, and I and other serious-minded golfers are not the victims of a hoax.

The nearest approach to this ball, with which we are threatened, was the old "Eclipse" which used to be made years ago by a firm in Edinburgh. I am an old enough golfer to remember it. It used to be called the "putty" as opposed to the ordinary "gutty." It was an ugly looking fellow of a yellowish color which had but little bounce it and went off the club, as somebody said, "like a thief in the night," with no cheerful ring. I remember very well when I was at school at Eton going to a photographer's shop in town—why a photographer should sell golf balls I do not know—and buying one golf ball with my last shilling. I could not understand why all my shots seemed to be half topped: I could not get that ball into the air and it was some little time before I realized that it was an Eclipse.

The ball had its triumphs. Mr. Horace Hutchinson played with it and won his first two Amateur Championships with it. In his "Fifty Years of Golf" he tells us something about it. "It was," he says, "indestructible. Then it was a wonderful ball for keeping its line on the putting green—far the best putting ball that ever has come into being during the half century of golf that I have known. But the quality, which perhaps was its highest virtue, was that it did not go off the line nearly as much as the gutty when pulled or sliced . . . . Of course it was possible to pull or slice the putty, if you played badly enough, though it did not take the act nearly as freely as the gutty . . . . It was a fine ball against the wind—it kept so low and straight. On hard ground it would make up in its run for its loss of carry. But . . . it was an impossible ball to stop on the green off a lofted shot—it would not take a cut when one purposely tried to stop it."

I seem to recollect that it was not a popular ball, in that even those who played with it did not get much joy out of it and sometimes felt even a little ashamed of it. And of course the professionals, who were ball makers, did not like it. Mr. Hutchinson quotes Old Tom Morris as saying with a twinkle whenever an Eclipse did find trouble "Eh, the potties—I thoeht the potties never gaed aff the line." At any rate it has been dead, buried and forgotten for many years now but apropos of this menace from the midlands, Mr. Hutchinson's account of it makes interesting reading.

Golf would certainly be a funny game if this unsliceable, unhookable ball came in. It would save the Green Committee a great deal of money since only the narrowest strip of fairway would be necessary; all lateral hazards would be at a discount and the game would consist in direct frontal attacks upon complicated systems of trenches across the course. If the Committee built anything in the shape of a small mountain there would be an outcry against the gross unfairness of a bunker more than ten feet high.

These are however, I hope, the idlest speculations, for after all we do play golf for fun and the greatest fun in golf is to hit the ball into the sky. It is better to have lofted and sliced than never to have lofted at all, and nothing could make amends, if we were never to see again the white ball "sailing with supreme dominion through the azure fields of air."

Prestwick's Final Open Championship

Our Open Championship cup returned here only on a flying visit and has gone back to America yet again in the most worthy custody of a most popular winner, Jim Barnes. He and Macdonald Smith played at Prestwick, and it seemed likely if one of them did not win then the other would. In the ordinary way I should try to give our impressions of the run of the play, but this time, since so much has been said here, and, I have no doubt, been cabled across the Atlantic about Macdonald Smith's trouble with the crowd, that I think I had better give the impressions of an eyewitness on that point alone.

Prestwick has always been a place of great crowds. It is near Glasgow and in the heart of a golfing country. It is a place where it would be wholly impossible, even if it were desirable, to exclude spectators. It is also a place geographically ill adapted to a crowd. There are very narrow defiles on it; there is a stream to cross twice, and there is the huge Cardinal bunker that stretches at one point half the width of the course and demands much shepherding of the populace.

At the same time the organization of this shepherding process is excellent. I know of no place where the members wrestle with their task so valiantly and so unselfishly, giving up all chances of seeing anything of the golf themselves in order to enable the players to get round in some measure of comfort. If they failed on the afternoon of the second day it was because their task was an impossible one. I have seen several huge crowds at Prestwick, but this, I think, was the worst and Macdonald Smith, because he was leading the field and because he started late, got the worst of it. But many of the things said of this crowd have been unjust. They were good natured and they meant no harm to anybody; but they were very keen and when crowds are keen the germ of running and rushing will infect them; and there were so many of them they could not get out of each other's way, let alone the player's way.

Of all the people in the world they meant no harm to Macdonald Smith. If they killed him they killed him by kindness and I can adduce one very solid argument in favor of that statement. A Scottish crowd is desperately patriotic. If an American Scot in the shape of Macdonald Smith did not win, then it was certain that an American Englishman in the shape of Barnes would win, and no Scottish crowd would hesitate between the two.

Undoubtedly poor Macdonald Smith—and everybody was very sorry for him—did have a most trying time of it. It took a long time to clear the crowd out of the way before every shot and the waiting must have been racking to the nerves. Also, if one of the players was not on the green, but somewhere near it, it was only with great difficulty that a narrow lane could be formed down which he could play his shot. The greens themselves were clear and as far as the putting was concerned there was nothing to complain of, nothing that any popular idol does not have to put up with. But there was a general sense of hurly-burly and scrimmage, a constant series of eddies and swirls in the crowd; constant accessions of fresh spectators and fusions with other and minor crowds that must have made it very difficult to play golf. That Smith had a terribly hard row to hoe is certain, but the hardship was one of degree only, not of kind. Barnes had a crowd, Compston had a crowd, not so big, not so obstreperous, but still enough to be disturbing. And what of all the lesser lights? They did not have crowds of their own, perhaps, but they had to struggle through other people's crowds who did not care in the least what befell them; and that is no easy task.

Everybody had a difficult time of it, though admittedly the favorites had the worst, and so when I read, as I do, that nothing but the crowd could have prevented Smith from winning, then I wish mildly to protest against an overstatement. If Barnes could take a 79, as he did in his third round, then I

really cannot see why it was impossible that Macdonald Smith
should take a 79 in his fourth round.

Mind you, although if's are the most unsatisfactory things
in golf, I do personally think that if Smith had been less ham-
pered by the crowd he probably would have won. He might
even have won quite easily. I have a great deal of sympathy
for him. But I do also say this, that other people suffered, if in
a lesser degree, and that the ground was so "kittle," and the
golf so difficult, and the strokes could slip away so easily that
there is no golfer of whom it could be said with anything like
certainty that, in the fourth round with a championship to
gain, he *must* be able to do a 78 or less.

I have a fancy that Smith lost at any rate some part of his
championship in the third round. He was playing truly magnificent golf and was all fours for eleven holes. At the twelfth
he seemed likely to get another four when he missed a holable
putt of six feet or so, ran past and missed coming back. He
finished in 76, but he had another six in the last four holes. If
that first and quite unexpected disaster had not befallen him
at the twelfth it is my impression that he would have finished
in a 72 or thereabouts and held so commanding a lead that no
crowd could have prevented him from winning. But there
again, other people had their unexpected disasters, too. Was
there ever a championship without one? The whole affair was
unfortunate and I doubt whether an open championship ought
ever to be played at Prestwick again. It will be very sad it if is
not played there. Prestwick is the original home of the championship. It was there that the peerless Young Tommy Morris
made the belt his own by three successive victories. But these
are not the days of Young Tommy. Golf grows ever more widely
played and nowhere more so than in this corner of Ayrshire
which is one huge golf course.

Humanly speaking, it is certain that the next crowd will be
bigger still. No stewards, no posts and no ropes—and we had
plenty of all three last week—can hold them. Golf can be altogether too popular.

Eccentricities on the Green

The other day I forgot my golfing manners in a lamentable degree. I was playing in a foursome and among the four was a friend with whom I had not played for some time. When he took up his position to tackle his first putt of the day I burst into a scandalous guffaw of laughter, for he had taken to turning his toes inwards in such a fashion that they met and formed the apex of a triangle and his back view—I was watching him from behind—was altogether two much for my gravity. Yet, he putted rather well and moreover he defended himself by more or less convincing arguments, saying that this crab-like attitude prevented him from swaying his body.

Afterwards it occurred to me that golfers as a whole had grown less eccentric or more self-conscious in their putting attitudes. I do not mean to say that we all stand up to the ball on the green in chaste, elegant and classical poses: I am personally all too conscious that my knees are as those of a very old, broken-down cab horse. But I do not think that orthodoxy is quite so openly flouted as it used to be. It seems to me that fifteen to twenty years ago there were several golfers of my acquaintance—and very good ones too—who did surprising things not seen nowadays.

I think it was in 1907 that Mr. Hilton, then at the height of his fame, took to putting one-handed with his left hand imbedded in his pocket and very well he did it for a while. One of the very best putters I ever knew, though not otherwise a great golfer, used to stand over his ball directly facing the hole, the ball midway between his feet, and putt backhanded with his left hand. At anything like a short putt he was astonishingly deadly. He looked as if he could never fail to do two very important things, to take the club back straight and to let it go through after the ball.

Then I remember the late Mr. J. A. T. Bramston, a member of the Oxford and Cambridge side which toured America in 1905 and, till he fell ill all too young, a grand golfer. He took to putting with one hand at the top of the leather and one right down on the iron. This is certainly an inelegant, but for a while at any rate, a very comforting method. The player feels a new-born control of the club and he is apt to follow through so thoroughly that ill-natured opponents sometimes accuse him of hitting the ball twice.

Mr. Horace Hutchinson at one time adopted something of this method, though Heaven knows he putted well enough like an orthodox Christian. At least he placed his hands a long way apart and was so thorough as to take some modelling wax or kindred substance and affix to the shaft two moulds of his fingers, so that he could attain to an absolute fixity of grip. I believe too, though I will not swear to it, that I once saw a golfer with projecting handle fixed at right angles to the shaft of his putter, even as are those of a scythe.

Then there was a famous lawn tennis player of an early epoch, Mr. H. F. Lawford, who used to fight out championships with the immortal Renshaw. He became a good golfer and used in certain moods to turn his back on the hole and putt at it between his legs. Of course there were all sorts and kinds of croquet mallet putters, but they vanished when an unsympathetic Rules of Golf Committee made them illegal.

Today I conjure up pictures of all the golfers I know and see in my mind's eye nothing but a dull and blameless procession. Yet stay! I can think of one, Mr. Denys Scott, brother of Mr. Michael Scott, who played so well for our Walker Cup side against Mr. Sweetser at Garden City.

He took some years ago to placing his left hand below his right in putting and became a much better putter ever afterwards. His prototype is to be found on the old minutes of the Bruntsfield Links Golf Club of some ninety years ago when it was recorded that "During the Evening the Secretary sang the following impromptu:

"Come, all you golfers, stout and strong,
Who putt so sure and drive so long,
and I will sing you a good song
About old Captain Aitken.
There is no golfer in our view
Who drives so far and putts so true.
With left hand down, his club does wield
'Tis ten to one against the field."

As it was not at all "a good song," however, I will quote no more of it. I am glad there is still somebody to putt like "old Captain Aitken." It is so dull and drab when we all try to do the same thing. I suppose we grow orthodox because we are afraid of what people are whispering behind our backs. We hear them sniggering even as my crab-like friend heard me. If a man stands on his head to putt, his method will only be justified with success. The moment he misses a putt or two, as is only human, the fickle would turn and rend him. If he is going to stick to his eccentric ways, he must put on the triple brass of indifference to public opinion, for his downfall will always be hailed with savage glee.

Moreover, we often have no real lasting faith in our own eccentricities. Years ago there was a delightful golfer who played at Prestwick and he had a little tiny putter about a foot long, which served him well. One day it played him false and then he seized and battered it against the stone wall that ran across the links, with these memorable words, "You little ____ ____, don't you presume on my good nature any longer."

In one of the earliest of golfing or presumably golfing pictures from an old Flemish Book of Hours, there is to be seen a small boy putting at an undoubted hole in the ground, while kneeling down on both knees. I often wonder why nobody has adopted his prayerful attitude. At least I have never seen anyone do so. Yet trying it on the floor of my room it seems comfortable. I am hitting the legs of the table with the greatest accuracy, though to the detriment of the already baggy knees of my trousers. Who will be a really brave man and putt on his knees in public?

1926

A Champion at 58

A vast number of middle-aged golfers on both sides of the Atlantic who were slipping consciously over the hill, must have taken heart again when they read of the last great triumph of the evergreen Sandy Herd. It is truly remarkable that a man who was born in 1868 should in 1926 win the Professional Championship of Great Britain by match play. It is a very remarkable thing and, in Kipling's words "makes you think better of you and your friend and the work you may have to do." After this a golfer of any spirit should be able to say with a single heart that a man is only as old as he feels, and go out and hit the ball to glory.

There are of course certain things that may be said in critical depreciation of this extraordinary feat. First it may be said that the young professionals should not allow such a thing to be possible. Well, perhaps that is true; in fact I know it is. At the same time Sandy was sticking to par golf or better all through those straining, struggling four days and whoever was going to beat him had got to go all out.

Then in the second place the ground was undoubtedly in his favor. In point of yards the Mid-Surrey course was very long indeed but the ground was so hard that it did not "play long" and Sandy, who in any case is far from a short driver, did not have to strive after length. It suited him to perfection since he is a past master of the art of hitting a ball with a slight draw which fairly fizzes when it lights and runs forever. He used that shot for all it was worth and it was as good as a play to see him wriggling his feet just a little more round during his multitudinous waggles in order to get just another little bit of draw and a few more yards of run.

I suppose too that the weather was in his favor since it was very fine and there was no heavy wind and no "blattering" rain to tire him out. Still when all that is said, his glory is undiminished, and not only did he win but so well did he play

102

that competent judges "tipped" him to win almost from the very start.

Sandy has always been a very great golfer, greater in match play than in score play, for the one Open Championship that stands to his name certainly does not do him justice. He is physically a very strong man; he has lived a most healthy and abstemious life; he has spared no pains to keep young by doing "physical jerks" every morning; and he has been professional at clubs where he has had constant opportunities of playing in good hard matches, so that he has never for a moment got out of the way of it.

But these things would have been of no value at all without his indomitably youthful spirit. That is his real secret; that he has never talked of getting old, hardly ever even thought of it. Seeing no reason why he should not beat the boys he goes out and beats them.

In the first round of this tournament he was having a very good hard match against a Scottish professional, Barr by name, who is, I should suppose, in his later twenties. At the seventh hole, Herd, being one up, turned to J. H. Taylor who was walking round with him and said "This young man is playing very well." It was uttered in a simple, kindly tone as if he would say "of course a man of fifty-eight ought to beat a boy of twenty-eight but he's really doing very well and I shall have to work quite hard to beat him."

And it is that spirit that carries him through. He still dislikes being beaten as much as he ever did. By that I do not mean that he is a bad loser for there is no more sporting and generous player. I only mean that for most people, as they grow older, defeat loses something of its sting and then, though they be happier men, they will never again be such formidable golfers as they used to be. Now Herd is still as eager as when he played in his first championship forty years ago. He has no notion of being beaten, if he can possibly avoid it. If ever hope sprang eternal in any heart, it does so in his.

If any evidence were wanted of this perennially youthful

eagerness it is to be found in the fact that the faults of youth
are, with him, still those of age. He was always a magnificent
fighter when he was behind. Did he not once win a thirty-six
hole match against Vardon—and a Vardon then at the very
zenith of his fame—after being six down at the end of the first
round? Where he used sometimes to fail was in holding a winning lead by ordinarily steady golf. He used to look a little too
far ahead, to be too anxious to make victory come to him
instead of letting her come in her own good time.

It was that same weakness that now and again peeped out
in this last tournament. He always started off like a shot out of
a gun, but there were nearly always some uncomfortable moments when victory was in sight. In the final he was five up
and let himself be pulled down to all square; went away again
to be three up and again lost all his lead; became dormie one
and was robbed a third time (it must be admitted through no
fault of his, but by a magnificent three of his enemy's) and
then went on to win at the thirty-eighth hole.

While the holes of his lead were dropping away—in the old
familiar words "like snow off a dyke"—he was anxious and ill at
ease; but when they were all gone and he had his back to the
wall then he fought like a tiger. And, if I know him at all, he
will not regard this crowning success as any excuse for taking
things easily; it will only make him keener and harder to beat
if possible than before. He will be planning how to celebrate
his sixtieth birthday by winning again.

The Spoon Is
Only a Brassie

Some of those who read the account of the first day's play
in the University match may have found in one paragraph
food for thought, and perhaps even a clue to the improvement of their golf. This paragraph stated in effect that, after
the foursomes, J. H. Taylor had given Mr. Stephenson a severe talking-to on the subject of his "putter-faced" driver, and
had conjured him in impassioned language, for the sake of
Oxford and all that he held most dear, to put it away and
drive with a spoon (a 3 wood) on the morrow. Further, it was
stated in the account of the second day's play that Mr.
Stephenson had bravely bought a new and more lofted club
and had driven extremely well.

After the match was all over the master returned once again
to the assault of the pupil. The emphasis and kindly fury of his
words I cannot hope to convey, but the mere form of them I
can roughly reproduce. The pupil was not only to put his drivers away; he was to burn them; he was never again to let himself be seen in the master's presence with a driver in his hand
under nameless but obviously fearful penalties. Finally—and
here came a piece of encouragement as strategic as it was
kindly—he (the master himself) could not get the ball up into
the air with a putter-faced club.

I, too, was encouraged, as I listened, although the smile,
which always had a tendency to appear after a Cambridge victory, was wiped from my face by sheer awe. During a long and
ill-spent golfing life I have been driving with a brassie (a 2
wood) and have suffered from something of an "inferiority complex" on that account. When I was quite small I remember to
have been a little cheered by hearing that the great Mr. John
Ball, jr., drove with a brassie; but I gathered that he was an
eccentric genius who could not be bothered to carry two clubs

105

if one would do tolerably well. And then when at last my eyes beheld my hero he was using a driver, and there was no comfort left at all.

Of late years, when the inferiority complex has, as it were, settled down and got its second wind, I have observed with mild satisfaction that many eminent persons, and in particular the Americans, drive with brassies. These are not, indeed, brassies of my own old-fashioned type, but they have at least a neat little triangle of brass affixed to the sole of the club. Even so, to hear an inability to get the ball up spoken of by the truly great as no more than an amiable weakness was most reviving, and I feel it a duty to pass on the glad tidings to fellow-sufferers.

Let me further pass them this cheering hint. Unkind people who write in the newspapers, being in a hurry and wanting only to convey results, are apt to say that Mr. So-and-So "topped his wooden club shots." We are apt even to say it of ourselves. We must never do so again. Let us say rather that our style of play is to "hit the ball down." That sounds much better, for do not learned men in learned books tell us this is the way the ball should be hit? Moreover it is true that many a ball that is called topped is not topped but "smothered," and some loft on the face of the club is a sovereign preventive of smothering.

Anybody who has ever tried to coach a beginner must sometimes have observed that his or her whole manner of swinging became freer and better with a lofted club. We are not now beginners, but we retain something of their weaknesses. In our subconscious mind, if that be the right phrase, there is always the fear of the ball running along the ground. When that fear is stronger than usual our swing goes all to pieces and becomes a hurried snatch; when it is wholly absent we "wait for the ball" and hit it.

The spoon is today a very popular club, for the simple reason, as I believe, that it has an open and encouraging countenance. People are prone to talk about the spoon as if it possessed some mystic qualities. I am prepared to admit that some rare artists—Mr. Hilton, Duncan, and Herd are three obvious names—can juggle with it. Only the other day I played with an amateur of something lesser fame but of great ingenuity and accuracy, who said he was a happier man since he had taken to playing his mashie (5 iron) shots with a spoon. These are, however, exceptional cases.

For the general ruck of us a spoon is only a brassie with a more lofted face and a spoon shot is only a brassie shot hit rather higher, cleaner, and oftener than usual. Such at least is my own case, and if I took a spoon more frequently from the tee I should get into fewer troubles. To do so is rather a confession of weakness, a little akin to scuffling the short putts in with a mashie; but, after all, "better be a coward for five minutes than a dead man all your life." And then again there is a good deal in a name. We need not say that we are driving with spoons. We can say that we like to have the faces of our wooden clubs just a little set back.

The Waggler—
Past and Present

A few days ago, in a tournament of some little importance played in the south of England, there was one competitor who aroused some indignation in the hearts of those who played behind him, and a combination of curiosity, amusement and sympathy in those who watched him. Beyond all question he was the champion waggler of the world. Persons of a statistical turn of mind took the trouble to count and they professed to record as many as ninety (some indeed made it a hundred) addresses to the ball upon one tee, and fifty was nothing at all out of the way, whether on the tee or through the green. Some people disputed these figures on the ground that the forward and backward movement of the club constituted but one waggle, whereas the statisticians had counted them separately. This raises the difficult question of defining a waggle.

At any rate the poor man did take a most unconscionable time. His first adversary stood up as long as he could, then he sat down and lost the match. The second took out a shooting-stick to sit upon and he won. It was a case in which one felt sorry for both parties because it was clear that the waggler's waggles were beyond his control. He did his best, but he *could not stop*. I suppose all of us have at times had this disease in a very much milder form, but this was something altogether beyond a joke; it really was a disease.

I once knew a man who had one equally distressing, though of a rather different kind. He could waggle freely enough but when he came to put his club down behind the ball for the last time, then he stuck fast. Something stronger than himself utterly refused to let him move the clubhead. He thereupon consulted a doctor learned in "suggestion," and when it was suggested to him that there was really nothing to stop him from hitting the ball he went out on the links and drove like an angel. The cure was not complete at once, he had his ups and downs afterwards, but the disease gradually disappeared. He was luckier than another golfer of my acquaintance who could get the club to the top of the swing but could not get it down again. There it stuck and to watch him was like seeing somebody pulling in vain at an obstinate bellrope or trying to open a recalcitrant window. He did conquer the thing partially in the sense that the club did not remain in the air forever, but it was such an effort that in the end—since he was growing old—he thought it wise to give up golf. I am delighted to add that he has been a much happier man ever since.

So far I have been talking of freakish things and players, but the ordinary waggle of the ordinary man is not without interest. That which interests me is the very great change that has come over waggling since I began to play golf. In those remote days most of the good players were Scotsmen and the Scots had a free, flourishing, bombastic waggle which made the clubhead tremble beneath a pair of powerful wrists. It was emphatically an athletic or gymnastic performance.

Those who remember the late Mr. Norman Hunter, who was one of the Oxford and Cambridge Society side to tour America, and subsequently played in a memorable championship at Wheaton, Chicago, during a heat wave, will recollect the tremendous and exuberant freedom of his address, in which almost every part of the strong, young frame took its share. There was the old Scottish waggle carried to its ultimate point.

The English golfers did it also, however, and nobody ever had a more delightfully florid movement of the wrists than Mr. Horace Hutchinson. Moreover, there used not to be anything that could be called a "standardized" waggle. Nothing, for instance, could be more characteristic than Braid's menacing little additional shake of the clubhead. Herd, of course, with his method of deliberately lashing himself into the necessary state of fury, was in a class by himself.

Now today the waggle is beginning to be standardized and American golfers have had a great deal to do with it. In their search for the best way of doing things, and their relentless determination to cut out all superfluous frills, they have devised a waggle which fulfills its purpose with the minimum of unnecessary movement. In the old-fashioned flowery waggle the player's body rose and fell like the waves of the sea and the same movement was prone, occasionally, to repeat itself in the swing. What I take leave to call the American waggle produces no such tendency. I am sure, speaking as one who is too old to change bad habits, that it must be better, and the interesting thing is that practically all your golfers use it. At any rate, if I call up in my mind's eye a procession of American golfers all the pictures of the preliminary addresses are in effect identical—the swings make individual pictures, but the waggle—no; my mind's eye takes them, as it were, for granted.

Moreover, something of the same thing is beginning to happen here. We at any rate try to learn from our conquerors, and our young men, especially as it seems to be in Scotland, are cultivating this uniform and immobile waggle. Take two young Scotsmen, Mr. Jamieson, who so surprisingly beat the great Bobby, and Mr. Simpson, who beat Mr. Jamieson and then fell before Mr. Sweetser: neither has a trace of the old St. Andrews waggle and flourish. Both hold their bodies still and make one or two gentle passes with the clubhead behind the ball and not over it or in front of it.

Moreover, whether or not as an indirect result, their swings are much calmer than they used to be. There is a tradition that "Young Tommy" Morris used sometimes to break the shafts of clubs merely by waggling them. To be sure the shafts of those days were frailer and more tapering than are modern ones. However that my be, those heroic days are gone forever.

110

1927

The Guttie

In 1902 the rubber-cored ball replaced the gutta-percha ball, known as the "guttie." This new ball, invented by an American, Coburn Haskell, helped to transform golf. It was less expensive and went much farther than the guttie. By 1927, when this article was written, most golf courses had become too short for the rubber-cored ball. Jones complained that he was tired of driving and pitching on every hole. Sound familiar? It's precisely the same problem golf has today, 70 years later. Darwin discusses a possible solution for championships and other important competitions: the re-adoption of the guttie ball. The guttie was preferred by Vardon, Darwin, and many other fine golfers. A golfer could do many more things with it if he had the artistry. They believed the guttie made the game more enjoyable.

American golfers have lately, I gather, been exercising their minds on the possibility of some reasonable limitations of the golf ball. Mr. Bobby Jones himself has been quoted as saying that he grows weary of playing hole after hole with a mashie niblick (7 iron). I know, too, that Mr. Fownes, President of the U.S.G.A., is in favor of something being done to prevent the ever lengthening drives, which bring in their train ever lengthening golf courses. Since, then, the question of limitation is in the American air, I think that some readers may like to hear of an experimental match played here at Woking in Surrey, a few days ago with a newly made guttie ball.

I ought to say that this match was in itself a genuine match and not a piece of propaganda. A certain number of golfers, some twenty I think in all, of whom I am a humble one, have founded the Guttie Ball Club. They were mostly bred on the old ball; they like a game which enables them to use their whole pack of clubs, and they purpose now and again to treat themselves to a game with the guttie ball. The team they put in the field for this, their first match, was certainly a distinguished one. Of professionals—for the Club consists of both professionals and amateurs—there were Braid, Taylor, Herd and Ray. Of amateurs there were Tolley, Weathered, Harris, Torrance, Hezlet, Gillies, Storey, and the rest of the team, if less well known, were more than adequately good players.

Matched against them was a side of competent golfers armed with an ordinary rubber-cored ball. I imagine that man for man the Guttie Ball side was some four or five strokes a round better than their adversaries. Woking is not a very long course but it is by no means a short or easy one. The course of the Country Club at Brookline is the one among American courses of my acquaintance to which I should liken it. It was not stretched by any means to its full extent. What I may call the middle tees were used and the day was practically a windless one. The singles ended all square, the Guttie men won the foursomes and so the whole matter by two points.

The ball used was not quite a guttie in the old sense of the term. It was a solid homogenous ball made out of the same material as is used for making the cover of the rubber-cored ball of today. It was not at all stony and was a far friendlier, kindlier ball to hit than was the guttie used in the last experimental game some three years ago. Everybody agreed that, as regards the sensation of hitting, it was a delightful ball to play with. Its one fault—and that a remediable one—was that it had been made a little too light. It weighed a barely twenty-four pennyweights, and the old guttie used to be perceptibly heavier than that. In the result it was highly susceptible to the smallest error in striking and was inclined to drift and curl away on small provocation. If there had been a high wind I think it would have become rather unmanageable. The next batch of such balls will be made heavier.

Opinions and memories varied a good deal as to whether this new ball went farther or less far than the old guttie did. Some eminent persons thought one thing and some another, from which I deduce that there was not much in it one way or the other. As to how far it went as compared with the rubber core, I shall say that it was about forty yards behind in the tee shot, and that in two shots the disparity was still more marked, but here again there was some difference of opinion. On some points everyone was agreed. It was a most agreeable ball to hit through the green with a wooden club; it could be picked up sweetly and easily and those who have habitually used lofted wooden clubs through the greens found themselves taking their drivers—a sensation they had never expected to have again on this side of the grave.

It was also very pleasant for pitching. To pitch the ball up to the hole with "stop" on it was perceptibly easier than with the rubber core. Incidentally when it did pitch it did not make a horrid dent in the surface of the putting green. As for putting, it was a little but not very greatly slower than the rubber core. Lack of practice seemed to tell more in this department of the game than in any other; many of the Guttie men never seemed quite happy with their ball on the green, but I do not think this was the ball's fault.

As an interesting and amusing day's golf, the match was an unqualified success. Some who came to scoff remained to pray. Conspicuous among them was Sandy Herd who arrived vowing that he was a fool to have promised to play and departed declaring with obvious sincerity that he had not enjoyed a day's golf so much for ever so long.

It will be extremely interesting to see what happens when we get made, as we hope to, a ball of similar material but just a little heavier. It was clear that this ball was not perfect but it marked a step on the road. It gave at least some notion of what the game could be with a solid ball. It is perhaps worth adding that nobody thinks—as I imagine at least—that it would ever be either possible or desirable to ask the golfing world in general to play habitually with such a ball. Golf is played primarily for pleasure and for the general run on mankind the game would be less pleasurable with this ball than with the modern rubber core. But it is, I think, possible to dream of championships and other important competitions being played with some such ball.

A Book Review

There has just come to me across the Atlantic a very agreeable present in the shape of "Down the Fairway," bearing a kindly inscription from the two authors, Robert T. Jones, Jr., and O. B. Keeler. I have written to them to say "thank you," and now I want to write something about their work. I am not presuming to review it for one reason because it will, I imagine, have been already reviewed in *The American Golfer*, but it may be allowable to say a word or two on how it strikes a reader on the other side of the water.

There is a sentence in the chapter on putting which seems to me to give, as it were, the clue to the whole book. "There's always that specter of the three-putt green. I had three of them that last round at St. Anne's in the British Open Championship of 1926. You don't forget those things, I can tell you." That's just it. Bobby does not forget those things and if by chance he ever does he has his recording angel, with a prodigious memory, to help him remember. He does not forget a single one of the horrible and excruciating things that must happen in any critical round of golf. The pleasant ones may be enveloped in a rosy and golden haze but the dreadful ones always remain with him.

His book gives the impression, and I believe it to be a true one, that no one has ever striven and agonized, suffered and sweated more over golf than has this wonderful golfer, who seems to take championships so easily in his stride. And I use that rather impolite word "sweated" in its literal as well as its metaphorical sense, because he tells us that he "always loses from ten to fifteen pounds in a championship of three or six days duration." Really it is a good thing that there are not too many championships or poor Bobby would be a living skeleton. To take the game so hard and yet to play it with such perfect temper and courage—that is perhaps the most remarkable of his achievements. That he can do so proves, I think, something which I firmly believe, namely that there is no one so formidable as the nervous player who can control his nerves.

Among the many things that pleased me in this book there are two in particular. I like Bobby for saying a kindly word on behalf of two golfers for whom I have a fellow feeling, the man who is inclined to be short with his putts, and the man who throws, or at any rate wants to throw his clubs away. It is comforting to find a great golfer who does not think much of "Never up, never in" and holds that it is often made an excuse for banging the ball past the hole, not in any genuine effort to hole a putt but merely to avoid the accusation of cowardice. There is something both ingenuous and ingenious in his argument. "Of course," he says, "we never know but that the ball which is on the line and stops short should have holed out. But we *do* know the ball that ran past *did not* hole out."

He is in favor of just reaching the hole "with a dying ball" because for such a ball there are "four doors," at the front or the back or at either side. I have no manner of doubt that he is right in his own case, because he always or nearly always hits the ball clean on the putting green. As regards the humbler ones of us there is just this to be said, we are not always short because we are cowards; we are often short because we do not hit the ball as cleanly as we intend. Wherefore in our case it may be a good thing to make some allowance for that painful fact, even if occasionally we go racing beyond the hole.

As to throwing clubs about Bobby does not say that we ought to do it or may do it and "except once in a while in a little friendly round" he has long since given up doing it himself; but I like him for admitting that it is human to want to do. "It always seemed, and it seems today, such an utterly useless and idiotic thing to stand up to a perfectly simple shot, one that I *know* I can make a hundred times running without a miss, and then mess up the blamed thing the one time I want to make it!—and when you feel so extremely a fool and a bad golfer to boot, what the deuce can you do, except throw the club away?" There is fundamental truth and if there be anyone who cannot understand that exasperation he may never make a fool of himself but he will always be a bad golfer.

It is interesting to find right through the book how much importance Bobby attaches to playing against Par and not against a human opponent. We over here—doubtless to our detriment as players—have never thought so much about par, but it is noteworthy that incomparably our greatest match player amongst the amateurs, Mr. John Ball, who won eight Amateur Championships, always played his matches on the same principle, namely that of trying to do the hole in the right figure and letting the other man go to the devil in his own way. It seems paradoxical but it is probably true that the way to obtain a great reputation as a fighter is to forget that you have an enemy—or at any rate an earthly one.

The Happy Golfer

Go out and watch a match in which Mr. Jones or Mr. Tolley is playing, and listen to the remarks among the crowd. You will hear a middle-aged golfer with a handicap verging on double figures, who can play many shots ill and none especially well, say something like this: "Ah! if I could only drive the ball like these young fellows, I could do the rest of it well enough."

And what he means, though he dare not quite say so, is that he could do it a great deal better than they can. It is a delusion, of course, since he forgets that one of these young heroes can pitch like an angel, and that the other can putt like a fiend; but still it is a pleasant delusion and does nobody any harm.

I have lately been falling into this sin of covetousness while playing with a friend of mine. He is not a champion. Far from it indeed, for I can give him strokes, and yet he fills me alternately with envy and rage. First comes envy. If I had the golfing gifts that nature has lavished on him, how would I not use them! Then comes rage, because he wastes them so criminally and then envy again, because he remains perfectly happy whether he hits the ball or whether he misses it, and never inquires into the cause of either occurrence.

Let me describe the game of this exasperating prodigal. He has, first of all, the nameless and priceless gift of making the club move fast. His driver hums like a hornet through the air. He can hit shots that the gods might envy. Sometimes they are long and low, sometimes long and high, and sometimes, alas! they are so short and so low as to bury themselves at his very feet. It is in keeping with the rest of his perverse genius that when he is driving against a hurricane, which reduced his adversaries to utter impotence, he will hit a succession of Braid-like "screamers," and, when there is a gentle wind behind him, such as would encourage the veriest foozler, he tops outrageously and persistently.

118

Then as to his iron play. He has the easy and commanding stance of an Open Champion about to play a "push-shot." There are the hands a little in front, just as the books tell us they ought to be; the feet would fit into exactly their right place on one of those mats marked out in white squares on which the truly great are photographed: purely by the light of nature he looks like a picture of one of the Old Masters. You would swear that the club would come flashing down, time after time, with mechanical accuracy; away would fly the ball—a masterful divot with it—low at first and then rising to fall biting its way into the turf. And do these things happen? Well, occasionally they do, and are a joy to witness.

In fact, as he comes nearer to the hole, he is so prone to the common fluff that among his intimates that particular shot is always named after him. I will call it colorlessly a "Smith," lest any susceptibilities be wounded.

It is no uncommon event for him to hit a magnificent drive to within a mashie (5 iron) shot of the green, and then play two or three short, sharp "Smiths" before he reaches it. When he does reach it, he will probably hole a very long putt, and so add one more to his irritating qualities by getting a half after all. The putting of such a player can be so easily imagined as hardly to need description. He always looks as if he were going to hole out: he always stands up and gives the ball a fine, free, fearless knock, except very occasionally when he plays a "Smith" with his putter, and his opponent's only comfort lies in the fact that sometimes the hole is in the wrong place.

History relates that once he did himself full justice with all clubs. He could pull or slice, hit low or high at will: he did not play so much as the ghost of a "Smith." And then, after those two wonderful hours, he relapsed placidly into his old condition, in which every round is "unrhythmic, patched, the even and the odd"; and, when he has dubbed once, he is quite likely to dub two, three, and four more times in quick succession. He does not know whence the inspiration came, nor why it went away again, and—confound the fellow!—he does not care.

Deliberate Lying

It is a constant source of sorrow to us that our scores in medal competitions are so consistently higher than those that we make in matches. For this we are apt to assign two reasons; first, that the holes are cut in malignant places on medal days, and second, that a card in our pocket has a baneful effect on our nervous organization. Both these reasons are good enough in their way, but there is a third which is better still. It is one originally advanced, I think, by some robust skeptic to account for certain spiritualistic phenomena; it consists in "deliberate lying by persons incapable of deception."

We are all honourable men, but the scores that we say we have done in matches we never really did at all. Nor is our lying confined to our own scores. Those of us who write in newspapers are more splendidly mendacious about other people's scores in public than ever we are about our own in private. In old days the scores in matches used to be called "approximate," and that blessed word covered a number of dubious putts "given" to the player. Today it is much more seldom used.

Sometimes we really do behave outrageously. In the *News of the World* tournament at Mid-Surry Herd and Ray both pulled their tee shots to the third hole into a horrid position on the edge of the copse on the left. Ray in looking for his ball trod on it, and at once picked it up, and the players walked on to the fourth tee. Nevertheless I read that Herd had reached the turn in a certain score—I think 36—whereas in fact he could have had no score at all. What he would have done at that third hole was a matter of pure conjecture.

That is an exceptional instance, but there is a genuine difficulty—nay, more, an impossibility—of giving the scores accurately in nearly every match that ever was played. What happens constantly is this: A and B are both some six or seven feet from the hole, A having played three and B four; A holes his putt and B picks up. Now what shall be B's score for that hole? It is invariably recorded as a 5, because the recording angels of the newspapers really are so angelic; yet no sane man would give B a two-yard putt; he would say, "Putt it out."

It may be thought from my severe tone that I believe myself to be truthful about my own scores, but I am under no such delusion. I have frequently caught myself lying not only about my own score, but also on an even more magnificent scale about that of my conqueror. In this last respect some people seem to be permanently unfortunate in running into opponents who are playing better than they have ever done before or since.

There is a golfer who, as far as I can gather, has never been beaten save by an adversary who went round in 69. I think—I really do think—that he approximates a little. And if he does, is it not an amiable weakness? Is it not better than the grudging spirit which says, "No, he didn't play well—I beat myself"?

Bobby Jones' Conquest of St. Andrews

I wish Bobby Jones' admirers in his own country could have witnessed the scene at St. Andrews when he rapped the putt of three inches into the hole that made him again our open champion. They would have realized that there is one respect in which Britain declines to be beaten by America, namely, in enthusiasm for Bobby.

It really was an astonishing almost terrifying scene. There were, at a conservative estimate, twelve thousand people 'round the last green. As soon as that last putt was holed, the crowd flung away stewards as if they were straws and caring nothing for anyone else who was going to putt on that green, stormed the slope. In a twinkling of an eye the champion has disappeared. "One moment stood he as the angels stand" and then, "the next he was not." He was just swallowed up. Either he or somebody else seemed bound to be squashed to death, but after what appeared an age, but was only a few seconds, he reappeared, borne aloft on willing shoulders and in turn himself bearing aloft his precious putter. His cap soon vanished, but after the crowd had surged this way and that with their load for several minutes, he and his putter were safely on dry land again,—not, however, before a rescuing party had set out from the clubhouse to save him.

There was another great scene when Bobby was handed the cup, but this time he was safe inside the clubhouse railings where he made his very modest and charming little speech of thanks and announced that he was going to leave the cup in the care of the Royal and Ancient Club of which he is a member.

These scenes of unexampled enthusiasm were, of course, evidence of a very great personal popularity, but I think they were also evidence of something else, namely, of a general conviction that Bobby was by so much the best player, that it would have been a shame and an outrage if anyone else had dared to win. For a visitor to be able to force that conviction upon the whole of an intensely patriotic Scottish crowd is an astonishing thing, altogether outside the power of any other golfer in the world.

I am not going to tell again at length the story of the four rounds which has already long since been flashed across the Atlantic. It differed from the story of most of Bobby's triumphs in that he made his own pace and led from start to finish. As a rule, he has come up from behind. This time he got in front right away with his 68, and then had to stay there. To those of us who were looking on there never seemed any real doubt that he would stay there, but to Bobby himself, I fancy, that this making of his own pace was a very exhausting business and that he would have felt the strain less if he had only begun to come away from his field towards the end of the third round.

There were really only two moments when he looked like being in the least pressed. One was on the second day—Bobby had reached the turn in 37, when we heard that Hodson had added a 70 to his first round of 72. That meant that Bobby had to come home in 37 for a 74, which would make him tie with Hodson. Thirty-seven home at St. Andrews against even a slight wind is very good golf, and he was not playing convincingly. However, he took himself by the scruff of the neck, came home grandly in 35, and kept a lead of two.

The other doubtful moment was at the beginning of the last round. Robson had gotten within four strokes of him and Bobby had started quite badly with five holes in 23. There was just a doubt, but a hole or two afterwards Bobby had begun to do his four threes in a row, and that was that, once and for all. All through the tournament Bobby's driving was magnificent—magnificently long and magnificently straight. If one thing more than another won him the championship it was his wooden club play. The two long holes at St. Andrews, the fifth and the fourteenth, are both well over five hundred yards long, and apart from their length, the nature of the ground makes them particularly hard to reach in two. The ordinary rank and file were working reasonably hard to get them in five a piece. Bobby himself could not quite reach the fourteenth in two, but his total for those two holes played four times each was just 33 shots. They gave him his great chance in the last round of gaining a clear stroke from lesser men and he certainly took it.

His pitching, on the other hand, was hardly up to his proper standard. Of course, he made many beautiful pitches, but he also made some downright weak ones; he was always inclined to be short with them, and once, on the last day, he fluffed one into a bunker in front of his illustrious nose.

But, if he occasionally pitched weakly, he nearly always saved himself by his putting. Now and again, being mortal, he missed a putt, but he holed a great many and his approach putting was a model of free, clean hitting.

It was a long putt holed—ten yards at least—at the second hole in the first round which set him off on his 68. That hole had looked like a disaster for it ought to be a four, and it seemed almost certain to be a six. He had drawn his tee shot slightly and had been trapped; he had failed to get out with his first effort, and finally, when he reached the green in four, he was a good long way from the hole. And then down went that priceless putt for a five, which was worth more than many orthodox, featureless fours. He never again came so near to doing a six as at that hole, and, in fact he went around the old course four times without a six, a thing that has never been done before.

It is no derogation from Bobby's wonderful score of 285 to say that the conditions were ideal for scoring. The plain fact of the matter is that the weather came very near to making a fool of the classic course. Not only was there practically not a breath of wind, day after day, but the ground was unnaturally slow and grassy after much heavy rain. Those who know the course will realize that it was not its normal and interesting self in these circumstances. It was dull golf, with all the subtlety gone out of the shots, and none of that variety which an ever-shifting wind usually introduces. A big drive and then a high pitching shot, with some sort of spade mashie (6 iron) played right up to the pin in the sure and certain hope that it would not run over—that was the story of hole after hole.

There were just two or three holes which gave the great player his chance against the merely good player; otherwise he could only assert his superiority by a slightly greater steadiness in the playing of obvious shots. Whatever had been the conditions—if it had snowed ink—it is my firm conviction that Bobby would have won; but a stiff wind and a faster ground would have made it more interesting to watch him do it. As it was, he did marvelously, but the battlefield was hardly worthy of the victorious hero.

Comparisons

I have found a large number of people over here interested in Mr. Jerome Travers' "informal ranking of stars." They display their interest both by talking and writing. Nobody criticizes it at all fiercely—indeed it would be absurd to do so, for Mr. Travers stated his opinion most modestly and added expressly that the first five on his list were "so closely grouped that it seemed like splitting hairs to separate them." I should sum up the comments I have heard by saying that everybody thinks it a good list but everybody also thinks he could make one even better himself.

Mr. Travers' list is as follows: 1-Robert T. Jones, Jr., 2-Harry Vardon, 3-Walter Hagen, 4-J. H. Taylor, 5-James Braid, 6-MacDonald Smith. It has been variously criticized. I read one gentleman (possible with a long white beard) who complained that Young Tommy Morris was not included. Well, Tommy died twelve years before the compiler of the list was born, so we may let that pass.

A more serious criticism is that Harry Vardon is not at the top, and indeed I suppose it is to British golfers a sort of mild blasphemy to suggest that anyone ever played as well as—to say nothing of better than—Vardon. This classifying is a dangerous business and, though most of us are classifiers at heart, I am not going to put my head into a hornet's nest. "You're both right, and you're both wrong" is the safe position that I prefer to take up in such disputes.

I may, however, point out that some of Mr. Travers' critics should read his words carefully again. "The six players of my time" says he, and those words "of my time" are very important ones.

The first five on his list are all players of his time in the sense that they have been playing big golf while he himself has been playing it and watching it. But they can hardly all five be said to be players of the same time. Vardon and Braid were born, so the books tell us, in 1870 and 1871, Hagen in

1892 and Bobby Jones in 1901. Between the first year and the last the gap is altogether too long.

When Bobby Jones had scarcely attained to his first pair of knickerbockers, and Mr. Travers himself was a schoolboy, Vardon had had his bad illness and done his greatest deeds.

Fine player as he has been since, he has never been so great as he was with a gutty. The rubber-cored ball arrived in this country in 1902 when Vardon was already thirty-two years old. I should much prefer to say of these two wonderful golfers that each was the best of his own time and leave it there.

Mr. Travers rightly points out that Vardon's putting is frequently below proper standard, whereas Mr. Jones is an "accurate and reliable putter." But when Vardon, in his youthful prime and before his illness, was spread-eagling all fields, he was not a bad putter. He may not have been a very polished one, and he put his seconds so near the hole that he did not seem to have much putting to do, but he did not putt badly. He was always a good approach putter and did not in those far-off days suffer from that sudden hitch or jump in the movement of his club which has since attacked him at short range. He could and did get the ball in and was at least a reasonably efficient putter.

When it comes to number 3 and 4 on the list, Hagen and Taylor, the same remark as to dates applies. Between 1871 and 1892 there is a great gulf fixed. It is easy to argue forever that Taylor never had quite the power and the hurricane brilliancy of Hagen, and which to my mind is more certain that Hagen never had Taylor's power of making no bad shots. It is much more to the point that the two have never met, and never could have met when both have been at their best.

It is not fair to press this argument of dates too far in favor of the older men. Those who hold briefs for the younger one have a right to use it too, to say that golf has come on so much in popularity, that the number of players has so greatly increased, that the competition is today more severe than it used to be. That is entirely fair even though it is impossible to appraise exactly the effect of that increased competition. The most we can say is that here is another difficulty in the comparing of generations.

I was discussing the question the other day with one of the most brilliant of professionals (he is not on that list of six). He is one of the most devout worshippers of Vardon and he was saying that Vardon's supreme strength lay in his power of playing wooden club shots up to the hole. He added that this shot has to a very great extent disappeared in modern golf, which is a statement of fact. He further added—and this is only a statement of opinion—that the best of the modern golfers never could have played that shot as well or nearly as well as Vardon used to play it with the gutty.

There I did not wholly agree with him. Let it be freely admitted that no one today can hit a brassie shot up to the pin as accurately as Vardon did, but then nobody today has the same chance of acquiring that art or the same compelling necessity for doing so. For my part I believe that the man who is the best of his generation could learn, if he had to do so, to play the shot that his predecessors played.

Another telling point was made by that great pioneer of letters and golf, Mr. Horace Hutchinson, who wrote me the other day. He is no longer well enough—more is the pity—to play or watch golf, but he has not lost his interest in it, and he had, like everyone else, been greatly interested in Bobby Jones' triumphs. In regard to the American habit—a very good one and a kindly one to the greenkeepers—of taking iron shots clean, he said: "They couldn't have done that on the old courses when the ball was, five times in six, in a small hard cup. It's all right when it is sitting on top of the turf." Of course he did not mean to say that Mr. Jones or any other modern player could not have coped with the "small hard cup." They could have done so at least as well as their elders. His remark, however, is worth quoting as a reminder that we must take the perfection of modern greenkeeping into consideration. And indeed, anybody who recollects the greens at St. Andrews as they used to be, bare and keen, and as they are, velvety and perfect, ought to want no other reminder.

For myself I think that one of the best things said on the question, (I am not sure who said it), is that there have been three outstanding figures, makers of epochs, in golf; first there was Young Tommy Morris, then Harry Vardon and now Bobby Jones. That seems to me to put the questions, so to speak, in the right perspective, to say that there can be no absolute best and that the most any man can certainly do is to be the best of his time.

A good many years ago now, I asked Mr. Leslie Balfour Melville, who in his youth played many matches with Young Tommy Morris, how he thought—making all due allowances—Tommy compared with Vardon, Braid and Taylor. Perhaps it was a silly question but it elicited at any rate a wise answer, for after reflecting a while Mr. Balfour Melville answered, "Well, I cannot imagine anyone playing better than Young Tommy did."

I shall never forget that answer and I am quite sure that if I live to be eighty and some young shark asks me about Bobby Jones, I shall plagiarize shamelessly from "Leslie" and reply, "Well, I cannot imagine anyone playing better than Bobby did." Nor can I, and in defiance of those principles of caution and moderation that I have been so carefully laying down, I will now add that I do not believe that anyone will ever play better.

In my heart of hearts I don't believe that anyone will play as well!

Card and Pencil Golf

A few days ago, in company with some of my fellow-members of a golfing society, I went down to the seaside for a week-end. We were to play in a medal round and there were several very agreeable prizes for us to win if we could turn in a low enough score. The course on which we were to play is one of the best and pleasantest in the country, the weather promised to be perfect, we were all of us in good spirits, and having dined well—some of us beyond our means—retired to be full of delightful anticipations.

What a change there was in us next morning—the weather had fulfilled all our hopes, the greens looked velvety, but we were a hangdog crew;—

> Like the leaves of the forest when
> > autumn hath blown
> That host on the morrow lay
> > withered and strown.

As we drive from our hotel to the course we looked with dreary eyes on the sunshiny sea and the white cliffs beyond. Then said one heaving a deep sigh: "What fun this would be if we were just going to play a friendly game." "Yes," said another, "Fancy coming all this way to this lovely course to play with a confounded card and pencil!" And all the rest of us cried in chorus: "Why on earth do we do it?"

It is a question which I have often asked myself before and to which I have still to find any adequate reply. I have never yet set out on a medal round without feeling sick and miserable; I have never yet completed one without having felt during some part of it exceedingly cross; I have never yet heard of the postponement of a competition in which I was going to take part without a desire to offer a votive table or the appropriate saint. Nor do I believe these sentiments to be in the least peculiar to myself. But the fact remains that if there had

130

been no medal round and no prizes, if we had been bidden to assemble merely to play jovial and friendly matches amongst ourselves, we should none of us have come. The desire to acquire silver objects or to see our names in the newspapers must be deeply rooted in the human breast.

For my part I believe that the perfectly successful meeting can only be attained by guile. The prizes should be duly advertised, entrance fees paid, a time-sheet fixed, perhaps even scoring cards issued, and then at the very last moment the officials should announce that the competitions will not take place. With what a spontaneous outburst of joy and relief would those cards be torn into the smallest pieces! With what holiday faces would the players go out to their four-ball matches! I suppose everybody has had dreams of paying some day his periodical visit to the dentist, and after being duly pinioned and gagged and swung into mid-air, of receiving the intelligence that there was positively nothing to be done this time. Some of us have now come to a time when that vision has lost its poignancy; the dentist has done his worst—or his best—for us, and there are some things that can never happen again. But we can still imagine the ecstasy of that reprieve. It would have been heavenly, but not more so than would be the sudden remission of a sentence of card and pencil servitude.

Golfing Emotions

I have just been reading Mr. Jerome Traver's book "The Fifth Estate." It seemed to me most interesting as a study of golfing temperament. On this point Mr. Travers has much to say that is eminently believable because it is so clearly founded on his own experience of a temperament not naturally unruffled but coerced by sheer strength of character into an outwardly frozen calm. It may be that there is nothing entirely new to say on the subject but there is much that can be said in a new way, and moreover the things that are old we cannot say to ourselves too often. One of the very truest remarks of Mr. Travers, one moreover which he illustrated himself better perhaps than any other man is this "The key to winning golf is the shot which is being made. Think only of it—Think of its execution, not of its importance; and, above all else, forget any mishaps which may have preceded it."

If only we could all do that! At any rate Mr. Travers came nearest to doing it of any man I ever saw. No doubt fifty examples could be given but there is one that sticks in my head. I saw Mr. Travers win one of his four Amateur championships at Garden City in 1913, when he was hitting his tee shots with an iron, and when, by the way, he was wrestling with a severe attack of socketing his mashie (5 iron) shots. The most wonderful part of the performance to me was that in several of his matches, as soon as he had acquired a short lead, out came his wooden club again for yet another try. The lead as a rule then automatically vanished and out came the iron again. Now any other man in the world, once he had made up his mind to the iron, would, I think, have stuck to it. Anyone else would have found it altogether too unsettling to return ever and anon to the experiments with wood. The man who could do that must have had a tremendous power of forgetting all about what had gone before and thinking only of the matter in hand. I never saw that power as uniquely well demonstrated. Of the advantage of forgetting what has gone before I can give one very simple illustration.

Take the position of two up with three to play. Suppose we had reached it gradually and steadily after a continuously hard fight in which no one has ever had a long lead, we feel that we are on the edge of victory; neither slack on the one hand nor frightened on the other but quietly confident. But suppose that we have been five up with seven to play and have lost three out of the last four holes, how different and how unpleasant are our sensations. Our mind goes harking back to what might have been. If we had only kept steady, we reflect bitterly, we could have had the match won by this time. The two holes that are left to us seem but a very slippery rock of safety. Now if we had the perfect or nearly perfect temperament we should know no more than this, that we are two up with three to go and that this is a strong position. But alas! for most of us circumstances do alter cases so terribly.

Another very true remark of Mr. Travers is this "I am unconvinced that it is inborn stolidity that gives to the golfer the tranquil mind and the steady hand which propel the winning shot." I humbly and entirely agree with him. I do not believe in the type of man whom Jack White once described to me as having a "dead nerve." I believe in the highly strung man who can keep himself under control. I remember being told of one of the most famous advocates of the English Bar that even in a small case the papers rattled and trembled in his hand before he began his speech; once on his feet he was suavity and calm itself. That is the kind of nerves I want for my ideal golfer and here again does not Mr. Travers illustrate his own remarks? He was never stolid but he could hold himself in an iron grip. "Perhaps I was not quite so susceptible to the fidgets" he says "as most golfers, but now that the old reputation for coolness has ceased to be an asset I'll make the frank confession that time and again my nerves have been so raggedy that I thought they would never hold together."And yet they only once failed to hold together in all his career and of that occasion their owner gives a very frank and straightforward account when he describes how he might have won the British championship at Sandwich in 1914. Sleep and nerves suddenly forsook him just when he was at his best. It was just the exception to prove the rule that he was a mighty fighter.

Confidence

A little while ago I was playing in a team match with a party of old friends. Perhaps we were all a little too old— or too friendly; at any rate we played remarkably ill. On that point we were all agreed and when the match was over we all advanced a number of reasons to account for it. By far the most original reason was given by my own foursome partner. We had been dormie two; the other pair were not on the green in two; he had before him a fair and open space void of bunkers; whereupon he hit our joint ball somewhere behind the heel of his brassey and wedged it, wholly unplayable, against the trunk of a fir tree. Then in a perfectly placid, almost drowsy way that belongs to him, he remarked "Do you know I think I missed that shot from over confidence."

And I believe he spoke the truth though he is one of the very few people in the world whom I should believe if he said such a thing. As a general rule I confess myself a sad skeptic about over confidence. It has lost in my judgment very few holes. When I read in the newspapers that so-and-so missed a short putt "apparently through carelessness," I write down the reporter in my own mind either as an ass or a very charitable man. For one short putt that was missed through carelessness ten thousand have been missed because the putter was trembling with nervousness.

Similarly when a friend, seeking my sympathy tells me that he was four up in the first six holes and "then began to get slack" I may say to him aloud "hard lines" or "too bad," but what I say to him not aloud but in the recesses of my own brain, is something like his: "My boy, I am too old a bird to be caught with this sort of chat. You were anxious to finish him off in a hurry. You said to yourself that things were too good to be true, that they could not last, that something horrible was sure to happen soon," and happen, of course, it did.

Over confidence may now and again make us hit too hard. Beyond that I very much doubt if it ever did anyone much harm and the sermons that are preached against it are usually quite unnecessary. Sometimes it occurs that A, who normally gives B three or four shots, has to meet him on level terms in a tournament and to the general surprise is beaten. Was he over confident? I don't believe a word of it. He was saying to himself all the while "What a fool I shall look if I let this fellow beat me." I am quite an infidel on this subject and shall never be converted.

Confidence—real confidence—is just about the most valuable of all golfing gifts. It is not very easy to define but I think I know some of the symptoms of it when I am conscious of it. If, on one of these exceedingly rare occasions, I miss a shot, a drive, an iron shot or whatever it may be, I do not catechize myself as to what I did wrong or wonder if I shall do it wrong again next time; I simply accept the miss as an inevitable result of being a very frail or ordinary mortal. If my long putts are going tantalizingly near the hole without dropping I do not say "Heaven does not mean me to hole puts today," but rather "If I can keep on like this one of them must drop sooner or later." To turn from the humble to the illustrious, Hagen, the most confident of golfers, always seems to me to be playing on this principle, in the firm belief that chances must come and things even themselves out in the long run.

No doubt the most important evidence of confidence, or the lack of it, is to be found in the things that we say to ourselves; but the things that golfers say aloud are important too. Suppose that during a tournament you meet a golfer evidently well satisfied and ask how his match stands, it is a long odd that he will not tell you in precise terms. He will say "Oh, I am a hole or two up" or "I'm doing fairly well at present." He *may* be doing this to spare his adversary's feelings, but this is rare. That which is at the bottom of his mind is that he fears to bring some dreadful Nemesis on his track, by saying aloud exactly how many holes he is up. But now and again you will meet the man who says quite simply "I am four up." That is the man for my money, and, if he adds confidently "I think I've got him," my faith in him is still greater.

There is a little story that I always like about Colonel Sir F. S. Jackson, formerly Captain of the England Cricket eleven, now the Governor of a province in India, and one of the greatest game players in a tight place that ever lived. It was a crucial match between England and Australia. The first three English players, batsmen of great renown, had gone out for almost nothing. The cricket was bad, the Australians were bowling like demons and it was an occasion when anyone might fail. As Jackson went down the pavilion steps to bat he whispered to a friend "They've none of them got any guts" and promptly went in and played an inning which pulled the whole match around and won it for England. Now there was confidence in excelsis. He never thought what his friend might think or say, if after that bold speech, he should fail; he just felt that he could do it and he did.

There is this too to be said about confidence, that it does not consist in a purely selfish belief in ourselves. An important part of it is a reasonable disbelief in the enemy. How dreadfully well most of us know the feeling that the adversary is infallible. It comes over us when we have had a winning lead and frittered it away, so that our utmost ambition does not soar beyond somehow halving a hole. If at such a moment we could believe that which is a fact, that the enemy is of flesh and blood and may miss, we should yet win the match comfortably enough, but honestly to believe it is sometimes one of the hardest things to do in all golf.

1928

The Courage of Despair

I remember several years ago getting arrested on my way to a well-earned bed, with my chamber candle actually alight, by a friendly fiend who set me this question: "Would you rather play golf like Taylor or like Braid?" The candle had almost burnt down to its socket and my yawns were pathetic in their intensity by the time we had finished the discussion and I had shut him safely into his room.

It was assumed for the purposes of the argument that Taylor always went flawlessly down the middle of the course, whereas Braid occasionally erred with a mighty hook and then recovered by removing several clumps of heather with an equally mighty niblick (8 iron) shot. It is an assumption which I trust an old friend will not regard as defamatory. At the time, while recognizing all the splendour of the recovering school, I declared that, could my wish be granted, I should choose the blameless and monotonous way down the middle. I have remained ever since of the same opinion, but quite lately I was the witness of a series of recoveries so transcendently glorious and exciting that I am now inclined to change my views and my prayers.

It was only a very few days ago that I was playing in a medal round at Woking with a highly distinguished golfer. He is entitled, and more than entitled, to wear the tie of the Seniors Golfing Society, but being a man of quiet tastes, he seldom does so. I should like, briefly and imperfectly, since my space is limited, to give an outline of his play at the first four holes. His first tee shot, somewhat short, ended in the outskirts of the small copse to the right of the green. Thence he played a low, hard, running shot. The ball, as he remarked with an air as nearly aggrieved as is possible with him, did not touch a single branch, with the result that it raced headlong across the green and plunged into a horrid mess of heather far down the slope. He dislodged it with an extraordinary skillful shot; it reached the green and lay some ten yards from the hole, from which it was cut off by a number of puzzling slopes and counter-slopes. Bang! In it went and that was a par 4.

At the second, which is a long one-shot hole, he made my blood run cold by calling for his brassy (2 wood). What was worse, he hit the ball as clean as a whistle. Where it might have gone is still a matter of tremulous conjecture. What it did was to hit a tree on the left-hand edge of the green at about 100 m.p.h. and fall like a stone at its foot. He played a beautiful run-up which threaded its way between the tree trunks and holed a five-foot putt. Par 3. At the third his tee shot soared away far to the right over the holly bush; he hacked it out of the heather, banged his third against the bank behind the hole, whence it fell back spent and exhausted, and down went a four-yard putt. Par 4.

Now for the most exciting hole of all—the fourth, with the tee far back and the greedy railway on the right waiting remorselessly for a slice. The drive was all too perfect, long, and dead straight. So naturally it ended in the little bunker in the middle which is like the Principal's Nose at St. Andrews. Moreover, it was tucked up under the face, and the ordinary frail mortal would have dug it out a few yards and "trusted to a pitch and a putt." Remarking that he had not thought he could reach it, our hero advanced with placid ferocity to the assault. The ball hummed through the air, carried the green, and the bunker beyond it and the ditch beyond the bunker, and startled the players in front who were waggling in a painstaking manner on the fifth tee. A wonderful chip back, eluding as if by magic all manner of fir trees and gorse, put the ball within 6 ft. and then—oh! tragic and unaccountable circumstance!—he missed the putt and so was one over par for four holes, which would have meant a torn card for any meaner man. From that point he lapsed into comparative dullness and orthodoxy; to the joy of his partner and everyone else he won the medal, but he would have won it, I am sure, much more easily if he could have had a few more adventures.

I do trust that no one will think that I have described those four holes with any spice of malice, because I can say with my hand on my heart that I never admired any golfer more in my life. There never was a better example of fortune favouring the brave. The player who can crash into wooded horrors over a green and say, if he says anything at all, "I've gone too far," is possessed of rare and precious qualities.

Recovering is, to be sure, a matter of strength and of skill, but it is also a matter of something much more important—greatness of soul. There have been certain golfers, of whom the most famous example was the late F. G. Tait, who have had the reputation of being lucky. There is another somewhat less famous—his name also begins with a T—who is universally believed by all his friends to be the luckiest golfer in the world; and certainly his ball has seemed at times to my grudging eyes to have the qualities of Spring-heeled Jack. But I have never yet met a player reputed to be lucky who did not possess a light-hearted, uncomplaining courage and a power of believing in that which he knew to be impossible. Those of us who have not these virtues lose half the fun of a recovery when we chance to make one because we know in our hearts that we did not deserve it; we played the shot with the carelessness rather than the courage of despair. These few great ones can openly rejoice because they had always hoped.

A Wee Caddie

There is a certain gallant friend of mine—gallant officially because he holds his Majesty's Commission, and gallant in fact because he has been the hero of some of the most triumphant rearguard actions ever fought at golf. A few days ago he was playing in a Foursome. It is a form of the game in which he usually shines with peculiar lustre, but on this occasion he did not shine at all. As regards the first seven holes I cannot do better than give the simple and direct words of his partner, who said that he "could not function." He had a small caddie who was deeply pained at this display, but managed to swallow down his feelings in silence during those first seven holes. On the eighth tee the child could bear it no longer, but produced from his pocket a cigarette card bearing a picture of Abe Mitchell, thrust it under his master's nose, and exclaimed, "Do you see how he swings the club, Sir?"

To the earnest psychologist the most remarkable part of the story is the sequel. From that moment the player scintillated steadily. And why did he scintillate? Alas! I cannot answer my own rhetorical question. Perhaps he imagined that he was Abe Mitchell cracking the ball along with that murderous turnover of the right wrist. Perhaps the picture suggested to him the subtle something that he ought to do and had not been doing. Or possibly the mere fact of laughing at his small instructor changed the murky current of his thoughts and made him hit the next shot with a lighter heart and so a lighter hand. I do not know, and very likely he does not quite know himself. All that is known is that somehow he learned wisdom from the mouth of this babe and suckling and for the rest of the day, like the jolly young waterman in the song, he "played along thinking of nothing at all."

The Voice of the Rabbit

The voice of the rabbit is heard in the land once more. He does not resemble the cuckoo. In June he does not change his tune. His mournful song is ever the same. The holes, he says, are too long and so are the carries; the courses are laid out by tigers for tigers. He has been recently saying it again in a number of letters to the press.

Personally I have a great deal of sympathy with these rabbits. As one who is sloping slowly, or perhaps not very slowly, towards their condition I agree that courses and holes are often made wearifully long. Because I sympathize with them I do not wish to emphasize too strongly the fact that some of their premises are doubtful and weak.

They imply that it is only the good players who are the long drivers, but in fact there has arisen today a whole generation of golfers, all of whom can hit the ball a long way, yet many of whom are far from being good players.

They seem also to imply, in their demands that skill and accuracy should be rewarded, that these attributes go with short driving; but this is not so; the majority of short drivers have little skill, and their accuracy consists largely in being so short as to be unable to reach the rough. When all is said, however, I agree that many courses, at any rate when they are at full stretch, are not calculated to give anything like the maximum of pleasure to anything like the majority of golfers.

If this be so, where does the remedy lie? Surely in the hands of the rabbits. They are always telling us that they pay the piper. Then why don't they call the tune? There is nothing mysterious about the constitution of a good golf club, and "one rabbit one vote" is one of its most glorious and undoubted maxims. They have only to conspire in their burrows and then come to a general meeting, turn all the tigers off the committee, and play old Harry with the course to their heart's content.

That in fact they do not is due, I suppose, to two causes. In the first place they are lazy in organizing revolt, and in the second a great many of them from motives, whether noble or ignoble, like to think that their course has a reputation for being long and hard, especially longer and harder than those of their immediate neighbors. However that may be, until they do organize revolt, it is perhaps not unfair to suggest that they deserve to remain slaves.

It is my private impression that a soviet of red rabbits would lay out a bad course, so bad that they would either share the fate of most revolutionaries and be quickly turned out, or else would be compelled to get a few mild scratch players of democratic tendencies to come and strengthen them. The sort of person who would lay out a far better course would be a rather *passe* tiger brought up in the traditions of the elder Scottish courses.

I was talking to one such only the other day. He is not, I think, any older than I am, but his memory goes back into a dim historic past. He can remember Prestwick when it was a 12-hole course within the now departed wall. He held me enthralled as he spoke of days when men played to the Sea Headrig green (this is how he insisted with some acerbity that it should be spelled) from a spot somewhere near the road, when there was a green on the high plateau on the way to the Lunch House Hole, that is to say, the fifteenth. He told of a hole called the "Green Hollow" (what a delicious name!) short of the Alps, and he reproached me for talking ignorantly of "The Cardinal's Back" instead of "The back of the Cardinal."

This, however, was incidental. He only developed his views when I happened to allude to a certain course as having been in its inception laid out for the new ball. He looked at me with some disgust and said that my words had for him no meaning whatever. There ought to be no such thing as laying out a course for a ball.

The proper procedure was to chose a good place for a hole and a good place for a tee. Then you said to the player, "There is the hole. Get into it in as few strokes as possible and as best you can." I rather gathered that he would be all the more pleased if the getting there required some noble sacrifices from those who were short drivers. Certainly he would have no weak-kneed sympathy with the long driver who complained of being trapped from driving too far, and he would not think much of "good length" or "two-shot" holes.

He added that if he had unlimited time and unlimited money he would buy a tract of golfing ground, lay out his ideal course, which all the best players would deem an unfair one, and then tempt them with handsome rewards to come and play on it, while he chuckled over their grumblings. The rabbits would grumble but so would the tigers and that is a proper democracy.

Bobby Jones's Achilles Heel

I am conscious of being a little late with my article this month, though I hope I am not too late for the mail. I meant first of all to write after the Walker Cup Matches. Then there seemed so little to say I thought I would wait till after the National Championship. The championship has come and gone and now what is there to say about Mr. Bobby Jones? A kind friend once told me that he would read anything I wrote except on the single subject of Bobby. He was, he explained, tired of superlatives. If I avoid the pitfall of superlatives my work becomes still more difficult. Still I must try.

As to the Walker Cup Matches there is really nothing to say except that we were thoroughly beaten by a magnificent side which is a great deal better than anything that we can produce. As to Bobby, apart from the fact that I am delighted that he won, yet, again, I have just one remark to make. In the lean years of his waiting before he "broke through" and won the championship so long overdue, people used to say that his marvelously smooth and rhythmic swing inspired his enemies by its example so that they played better than they ever had done before.

And really there seemed to be something in it. Year after year somebody went unkindly mad against him and produced a quite unbeatable kind of golf. Personally I only saw it happen once. That was at The Country Club in 1922 when Mr. Sweetser played against him with inhuman and indecent brilliancy, but I gather that other people did the same thing, perhaps on a slightly reduced scale, in other years. Well, they do it no longer. When they meet Bobby today they play just as well as he allows them and they get beaten by something in the nature of 11 and 10.

No doubt Bobby is a better player now than in those waiting years. In point of cold fact he takes fewer putts than he used to and from a more imaginative point of view, he is not weighed down by the feeling that he is never going to win. He is happily conscious, and more and more conscious every year, of having given the ultimate proof of his greatness. Still he was a desperately good player in those old despairing days, good enough to win over and over again, and yet people could play brilliantly against him, Now, save for Mr. Von Elm two years ago, it seems that they cannot. They know he can beat them and they know that he knows, and that accumulation of knowledge is too much for them. His rhythmic perfection inspires them no longer; it cows them instead. At least that is how I read the psychological riddle.

I said I had one remark to make about him. There is just one more that now occurs to me. Mr. Tolley has been fluttering our golfing dovecotes here by declaring in print that if we want better Walker Cup teams, we must play our Amateur Championship by a qualifying round followed by eighteen-hole matches. This is a train of thought that I cannot wholly follow but I mention it for a purpose. It occurs to me that some day soon there may be a revolutionary movement in America in favor of playing the National Championship by eighteen-hole matches, not because it is the better way, but, out of sheer despair, because it is the only possible, if unlikely, way of preventing Mr. Bobby Jones from winning.

I am eagerly awaiting my copy of *The American Golfer* that shall give me full details of this championship, but without that I can see traces of that one slightly vulnerable point, that heel of Achilles, in the fact that Bobby won one of his eighteen-hole matches only at the nineteenth hole. I don't know whether he was dormy or whether he was all square with one to play, but at any rate it is clear that the match was what the great Duke of Wellington called the battle of Waterloo—"A d——d close-run thing." Looking at the championship as I did from a distance of some 3000 miles, I was thoroughly anxious and interested till those eighteen-hole rounds were over. When the thirty-six hole rounds began, my interest was academic. I knew what the end would be.

BERNARD DARWIN

In a story of Rudyard Kipling's there is an account of a jockey sitting perfectly still and happy, listening to the drumming of the hoofs, secure in the knowledge that at the right moment his mount will go away from the field to win at his ease. I was reading it again the other day (I cannot lay my hand on it now) and it reminded me of Bobby with the long trail of thirty-six holes in front of him, serene and confident, waiting to go away at his leisure and his pleasure.

The Right Box

My vanity, which is always receiving shocks, has just had a worse one than usual. I have been forced to reflect whether it would not be, in Mr. Serjeant Buzfuz's words, "more decent, more becoming, in better judgment and in better taste," if I stepped away from the back tees and played in future from those of the ladies.

The cause of so painful a doubt is my friend, if I may so term him, Mr. Joshua Crane, who has lately written an interesting article on handicapping in *The Field*. Mr. Crane sometimes makes us angry, if we take him too seriously, as when on the strength of a complicated system of marking courses he alleges that Gleneagles is much superior to St. Andrews. But after all he refuted himself in the most amiable and practical manner by taking a house at St. Andrews this summer.

I can only summarize Mr. Crane's remarks, which should be read in full. Briefly, he wants handicapping to be done not by the giving of strokes but by the using of different tees by different classes of players. His benevolent object, as I gather, is not so much to enable the weaker player to win as to give him the chance of playing a great hole as a great golfer plays it.

The long handicap player, he says, lives in a different world from the scratch man, and plays the holes by means of entirely different routes and strokes; he "can never know the joys of playing a legitimate four on the long fourteenth at St. Andrews nor even the seventeenth." Incidentally the examples seem scarcely the best possible, since it is hard to say what is a legitimate four at the seventeenth; the man who defiantly lashes his ball right home with his second between the bunker and the road might be said to have taken an illegitimate risk.

However, we may let that pass and cry "Hooroar for the principle." Mr. Crane goes on to point out what a joy it would be for this same long handicap player to "make a 74 at Sandwich even if it were from tees 60 yards in from of Hagen's." He

150

ends with an ecstatic picture of the humble one doing a 70 from these forward tees and boasting that he had played "for his strength and length exactly as good golf as Mr. Jones at the same figure."

Naturally there are objections, more or less obvious, to the proposal, and the first is this that Mr. Crane's system constitutes an unjustifiable admission that length is everything. That it certainly is not, but also certainly it is a good deal, if combined with any reasonable measure of accuracy.

Then there is a criticism that we should expect to hear from those who are, properly as I think, anxious to put some limit on the flight of the ball. They, or at any rate the more enthusiastic of them, might ask why the long handicap player should be deprived of one of his most enviable and glorious privileges, namely, that of playing brassie (2 wood) shots in place of the eternal mashie niblick (7 iron). These enthusiasts enjoy themselves immensely when they reduce themselves to a similar modest level by playing with a gutty ball, and exclaim, "O fortunatos nimium" of the old, the short, the fat and the slicey.

There is also an eminently practical difficulty in the shape of our common vanity. In a free country we can scarcely be dragooned into driving from tees that we do not like, and it is the sign of a very rare humility to go voluntarily to a forward tee when somebody else goes to a back one. If golfing society were entirely reconstituted on these new lines there might be consolations. You, or I might find it more titillating to our vanity to be scratch in the red tee box class than, let us say, six in the green box class; I assume, of course, that no number of variegated boxes could do away with all necessity for handicapping.

The horrid shock of being on account of age and infirmity moved forward to a humbler box might be compensated for by a drop in handicap. I know one course where there were two sets of boxes, and nearly everyone is perfectly content to play from those of the inferior colour; but then on that course the blue boxes do not denote forward tees; it is only that the

yellow ones denote back tees, and that, though the distinction may appear a subtle one, has a remarkably soothing
effect.

In cogitating over a proposal of this sort it is difficult not to
do so egotistically. There is, for example, that prospect of a
70-round at Sandwich which Mr. Crane dangles as a bait before my eyes. I try to imagine myself doing it. I picture myself
driving my very best from a tee suited to my condition and
Mr. Bobby Jones, so far off that he is only a speck on the horizon, driving from a tee suited to his condition.

I assume that by this beneficent arrangement we should be
playing our respective second shots from much the same place.
Even so, should I "for my length and strength play exactly as
good golf as Mr. Jones?" It may be that I am exceptionally
modest, but I doubt it. It seems to me probably that his mashie
niblick shots would end nearer to the hole than my mashie
niblick shots.

Certainly I should hope to do a certain number of 4's, but
would they be like his 4's? I am of opinion that they would
not. For my third I should have a long approach putt to play
or even a chip from off the edge of the green; I should not lay
it dead and with my fourth the ball would wobble in by the
back door. He would have a putt for 3; the ball would touch
the hole and remain 6 inches away, and I should say aloud,
"That will do, Bobby," and internally "Thank heaven for a half."

In that case I suppose that Mr. Crane would reply that I
had not yet found my right box in society and would push me
still further forward; but no—that would not do, because then I
should be out-driving my adversary, and should not be playing the same mashie niblick shot for my second as he was,
which is, as I understand, the consummation to be wished. I
am afraid I must give up the idea, alluring though it be. The
fact is that most of us will never know what it is to feel like
Mr. Jones, not even if we drive from tee boxes of gold and
silver set upon the very verge of the next green.

The Greatest
Golfer In the World

A number of expert golfers, including Bobby Jones and S. L. McKinlay, felt that Joyce Wethered was as Jones put it: the best golfer—man or woman—he had ever seen. She won the British Ladies' championship four times and retired from competition, like Jones, at the age of twenty-eight.

I am writing these lines on the day succeeding the dinner of the Royal Blackheath Golf Club, which, as all the world knows, is the oldest golf club in the world. It plays alas! no longer on the storied heath where we are taught to believe that King James I first played his strange Scottish game with his Scottish courtiers. It has only an ordinary though very pretty course in a suburban park, but it sill retains all its ancient customs and with them, as is only proper, a good conceit of itself.

So at this dinner we were ushered into the dining room by a piper in full rig. So was the haggis when it came in due course, the piper in front looking proud and splendid enough, two waiters in their dingy dress clothes following behind with bottles of whiskey, looking self conscious and anything but splendid. Then we all drank in turn from the old silver quaich as from a loving cup with our neighbors on either hand standing up to guard us as we drank.

Finally there was a great procession of past captains in their red coats (with the piper yet again) bearing aloft the silver club that was presented to the society in 1760. They filed with solemn and steady step round the room leading the new captain to his place, and when he got there, there was read to him an admonition that he should ever maintain all the rights and dignities of the club, and he forthwith kissed the silver club in token that he would do so.

As I watched all these pleasant things happening I could not help thinking of the old Blackheath golfers of a hundred and fifty years ago who played their rounds and drank their marriage noggins and ate their delicious turtles "with plenty of green fat," a present from Tobago, and did all the other agreeable things that we read of in the old minutes of the club. I imagined myself for a moment dining with them and not with their modern successors. I wondered what they would think of me, if I told them that I had just spent the day watching a mixed foursome tournament; that there was a young lady taking part in it who would drive all their venerable heads off, and that, if she entered for our Men's Amateur Championship, she would come very, very near to winning it. What would those astounded old gentlemen have thought golf was coming to and indeed what is Miss Joyce Wethered's golf coming to? It was good before but it seems to me to have got quite a lot better since she retired from the championship arena. I have never seen any woman's golf in the least degree comparable to what it is now.

This very afternoon—it was in the semifinal—I saw her and her partner beat another couple, who fought very gallantly, by three and two. "Hard luck," said I to the defeated man on the other side. "You played very well." "Well," said he, "we were just outplayed. She is the best golfer in the competition."

That may sound absurdly extravagant praise because Roger Wethered and Cyril Tolley were playing in this tournament to say nothing of various people who have played in our Walker Cup sides. Yet, upon my word, I don't think he was wrong. Miss Wethered has done something to her driving; she has added a little more sting to it and a little bit of draw which she controls to artistic perfection and she is now not a long woman driver but a long man driver.

I have seen her in this tournament splendidly outdriving some quite strong men golfers and as far as I can see the really big hitters such as her brother Roger only gain ten to twelve yards on her, when both hit their shots. As she practically never fails to do that, as she is an admirable iron player, a very steady putter and hardly knows the rough on the course by sight, she is, you will perceive, a difficult person to beat. I have played with her and watched her for seven or eight years now, but I have never seen such golf as she is playing now.

She has the true champion's ability to make a thrust that cannot be parried at the crucial moment of the battle. This very afternoon she and her partner were visibly struggling, already one down going to the seventh hole—a one-shot hole of one hundred and ninety yards. There was "a nipping and an eager" breeze against the players and, for any mortal, the shot required a full wooden club. The opposing lady played such a shot to perfection, and her ball ended six or seven feet short of the hole. One would have thought it an impossible shot for any golfer in the world to follow. Miss Wethered took her spoon, hit the ball so that it flew straight into the wind's eye without wavering an inch and ended nine inches from the hole. No mere words can convey the devastating nature of that thrust at that moment. The other side perceptibly crumbled under the blow and lost three or four holes in a row. They recovered afterwards, but it was too late. The mischief had been done and that one terrific shot had done it.

I wish my ghostly old gentlemen from Blackheath could have revisited the earth just to see that shot. When they first heard, in the Elysian Fields, of women playing golf they said no doubt in words of old George Glennie "No gowf at a'—just monkey's tricks." If they had seen that shot, however, they would have been converted once and for all.

Go to the Best Doctor

I am quite sure that most of us do not go often enough to a golfing doctor. I am equally sure that when we do go we ought to go to the best. What we in fact do is to say to anyone who happens to be playing with us, "I say, just tell me what I am doing wrong." He tells us the first thing that comes into his head; we do not really believe in him but give his cure just one half-hearted trial, and our last state is worse than our first.

Such at least is apt to be my own slip-shod habit in respect to medical advice. The other day, however, being in a more lamentable state of play than usual, and being lucky enough to be playing with one who is at once a great golfer and a great golfing doctor, I seized my golden opportunity. I begged him to tell me how I might be saved and promised him unreasoning and implicit obedience. After my first bad shot, which was not long in coming, he whispered one brief counsel in my ear, and behold I was instantly as a creature transfigured, doing threes and fours and then went twelve holes in goodness knows what.

Now what I want to know is exactly how much credit of these twelve holes—and some other quite respectable rounds that I have played since—will go to my doctor on the day of judgment. He is an extraordinarily acute observer and I am sure that his diagnosis of my malady was the correct one. But shall I not get a little of the credit too because I had so much faith? If I had not believed in him completely I suppose his words would have had but little effect. As it was my faith was so great that had he advised me to play standing on my head I believe I should have made some show of hitting the ball.

That is why I say we should always go to the best doctor we can find. Not only is his prescription likely to be the best, but still more important we shall believe that it is. As a very famous professional said to me the other day, "It does not take much to bring confidence back to the game. Just hit two or three shots and off you go." The converse alas! is also true, that it does not take much to take confidence away, but that is only a gloomy parenthesis. My point is that a golfing doctor who can give one confidence enough to hit just those two or three shots, may be worth untold gold.

My doctor, on this occasion, was an illustrious amateur, but I recollect another on which I besought a many times professional champion, almost with tears in my eyes, to tell me how to drive, and in about five minutes the trick was done. A lesser man might perhaps told me the same thing, but I doubt if he would have had the same effect. I might have wanted to argue with him or to say desparagingly, "Oh yes, but I've tried that before and it's no good to me"; and then, of course, it would have been no good.

There is another thing I want to know about my latest cure. When I parted from my doctor with heartfelt thanks he said, "You'll be all right as long as you remember." Now I want to know whether he meant that literally or whether he only meant generally to cheer me. I think the latter because though I have in fact been more or less "all right" it has been rather by forgetting than by remembering. What happened to me was what has happened to thousands of golfers. I remembered all too well. I, so to speak, doubled and trebled the dose of my medicine until it began to poison me. Luckily I found it out in time and figuratively put the medicine away on a shelf for a while. But the good it had done me still survived because that blessed confidence remained.

Whatever else one does I am certain of one thing that when one is sick in a golfing sense one should not apply for advice to another sick man. Mutual doctoring is of no use at all. I remember some years ago going out to play some holes with a friend. He said he could not hit the ball, so we agreed to go out and help each other. A more dismal failure could not be imagined. The hopelessness of the situation was apparent from the moment our first two tee shots were struck. Both might be termed reasonably good ones in the sense that both were of a fair length and both ended on the fairway. "Well," I said to my friend "that was a good one of yours anyway." "That cursed hook again," he growled in reply. "If I could hook a ball like that," I snarled angrily, "I should never grumble any more." "Why dash it all," he positively yelled, "that's the very thing I wanted you to cure." And so we went on. That which I called my loathsome slice he called a nice little drift to the right which kept the ball safely in play; and the hook which I en-vied him so bitterly made him foam at the mouth with rage.

It was just the same with the rest of the game. I was playing my pitches pretty well and putting contemptibly; his iron play was absurd but he was holing everything. Each of us told the other that if he would only go up to the ball and hit it boldly all would be well. I must add that we were still friends at the end of the round but medically we had certainly done each other no good.

In books, ladies, when in private, are alleged always to talk about each other's maladies and to enjoy it immensely. I do not know if this is true but it certainly is not true of men and golfing maladies. The fact is that when we are slicing our-selves we are utterly selfish; we do not care a row of pins about other folk's slices, not even those of our dearest friends. When we are in robust golfing health, however, when a slice seems impossible and the easiest thing in the world is to crack the ball down the middle, then we are not without sympathy for the less fortunate and are prepared really to try to discover what is the matter with them. I do not say that on that ac-count we shall be good doctors because we are willing ones. On the contrary I think that those golfers with the real gift of healing are very rare, which is all the more reason for seeking out the best when there is healing to be done.

Hagen at Sandwich

Once again British golfers have to take their hats off to Walter Hagen. He has played in our Open Championship seven times. Once he has been third, once second, and three times he has won. This is a great record and this third victory was at once the greatest and the most popular of the three.

It was the most popular because everyone appreciated the simplicity and cheerfulness of good sportsmanship with which he accepted his monstrous defeat a week earlier in a match at Moor Park against Archie Compston. Compston beat Hagen 18 and 17 over 36 holes, and it was Compston's greatest single victory, and he had a good many important victories under his belt before that. The courage with which Hagen refused to let himself be crushed by such a defeat, and the way he set immediately to work to recover his fitness and his touch—in short, his game—showed what a strong character he possessed. It was an example of truly amazing recuperative power and what we here refer to as "pluck" and pluck is a quality that everyone British reveres.

It was his greatest victory apart from these considerations, because, to my mind at least, he played the best golf he has yet played here. There was none of the patchiness that marked his golf at Hoylake, the downright bad streaks followed by brilliant spurts. He began with a steady round that kept him well in the running and then went from strength to strength, improving with each round. He did not have a single six in the course of his four rounds and it was this more than anything that won him the championship. His rivals did have sixes. They made a bad shot and then, if I may so express it, threw good money after bad.

Hagen made his bad strokes, too, but the next stroke was always a good one, either to make up for the bad one or at any rate to cut his loss and prevent any serious calamity. It was to my mind, this unique power of forgetting a bad shot and doing the very best possible in the situation in which he found himself, that put Hagen in the end two strokes ahead of Sarazen. I can think of at least two holes at which Sarazen, having made one bad shot, at once followed it up with another, and two shots was the margin that divided the men at the finish. Sarazen is a truly grand little golfer, but he has not yet got quite the indomitable patience of Hagen, or, so at least I read the riddle.

With eighteen holes remaining, there were now four men in it: Hagen 220, Sarazen and Jurado 221, Compston 222. Poor Jurado broke down early. Having been driving magnificently he got under two consecutive tee shots and found sand each time. 4 and 3 became 5 and 5, and that was the end of him. His chances just oozed away and though he came home splendidly, an 80 had thrown him clear out of the hunt.

Hagen came next and never have I seen him look more determined. Things did not go too well for the first seven holes. At the end of them he had dropped at least two strokes and could not afford to drop anymore. The eighth is a one-shot hole over a famous bunker called Hades. Its bark is worse than its bite, for it has a big open green with kindly slopes that sometimes sends the ball curving round to the hole. Hagen put his tee shot fairly near the hole and bang! in went his putt for two.

From that moment he looked like a conqueror and the crowd seemed to feel instinctively that they were watching the winning round. He had some luck at the ninth and again at the eleventh. In each case his ball lay in between two bunkers when it might just as well have been in one of them. But I think he had been rather unlucky in his earlier round and had some good breaks due to him. At any rate he got them and reeled off the next four holes in four apiece.

At the long fourteenth, where he could just have got home in two, he was bunkered and took five. At the fifteenth he was bunkered again, played a shot of astounding audacity in taking a ball clear from under the face when any ordinary person would have "exploded" it out and holed his putt for four.

After that, all was comparatively plain sailing and he finished perfectly with three par holes for his 72 and a total of 292.

By this time Compston and Sarazen were away in the distance at the far end of the course. Compston needed a 70 to tie. Sarazen a 71. Both were difficult tasks but, since the wind had dropped away to nothing, not impossible. The news soon filtered through that Compston had hooked a couple of tees shots and taken 37 going out. That killed him, and though he played valiantly all the way home, 73 was the best he could do.

Sarazen still had a chance, for some time a really good chance for he began with six holes in 23. A six at the long seventh was a setback and he turned in 36. That meant a 35 to tie—it was almost too much to ask for, with three long holes and only one short one in the homecoming nine. He played very well and his approach shots lipped the holes but the ball would not drop and so with Hagen looking on, the calmest person to all appearances in the whole crowd, he finished in 73, two shots behind Hagen.

The Beginner

The golfing beginner is not so common a phenomenon as he once was. There are indeed plenty of people whom one might mistake from their methods and results for beginners; there is no dearth of them, but these are golfers with a handicap of twenty-four or more, which is a different matter altogether.

Now and again, however, the genuine article may still be found, and I have every reason to suppose that I lighted on one the other day. I first saw him after walking through a hedge to the next tee. He was then about one hundred and fifty yards ahead of us, and his subsequent history made it appear a problem of some difficulty as to how he had ever got so far.

On that I can throw no light. I can only state what I saw with my own eyes. Five consecutive times—for I counted them and towards the end I am afraid I did not count in whisper—he missed the globe. He missed it by quite a large margin, and between each beating of the air he indulged in an elaborate wiggle, something in the style employed by Mr. Punch when he beats the policeman. Afterwards his progress, though still inconsiderable, was perceptible; he was improving, and if only on that account I believe him to have been a beginner, because it is the rare and blessed privilege of the beginner to improve.

He did not move me to laughter nor yet to wrath, for he was a kind man and allowed us to pass, but he did move me to jealousy. He could improve—there was the bitterness of it. Bicycling is at best a dull business, and against the wind an abominable one, but can we not all remember how heavenly was the first unaided wobble, when we found that our supporter had relaxed his hold, and that, without knowing it, we were going by ourselves? If I could remember beginning golf, which I cannot, I am sure my sensations must have been equally ecstatic.

And that misser of the globe—O *fortunatus nimium*— had got all that joy before him. "Oh yes," he would presently be saying with conscious pride, "I did loft it that time." He had not chronic faults; his right knee did not duck nor his right elbow fly into the air. He could not possibly get any worse, and the whole beautiful world lay at his feet.

I reflected sadly on what I would do if I was in that gentleman's place. "All print was open to him," as Mr. Boffin said enviously of Silas Wegg, but I decided that I would not avail myself of that privilege. I would not bemoider my mind with books about golf. On the other hand, I would have lessons. I would not aspire to one of the very "highbrow" golfing teachers, lest he should frighten and confuse me by talking too much and too learnedly about my hips. Rather would I seek out some one brought up in a simpler school who would just set me to swinging and swinging over and over again, telling me soothingly not to mind when I missed the ball, and throwing in now and again a word about slow back or the eye on the ball. Heavens! how I would toil and strive to do what he told me, and I believe he would make something of a player of me. And of course I should openly and proudly proclaim myself a beginner. That used once to be a not dishonourable name, entitling one to some kindly consideration.

163

1929

Cures and Cathedrals

I have received a letter from an American friend of mine, a very good golfer, whom I hope soon to see again in the flesh. He has lately landed here with his family, and they are engaged in touring England in a motor-car. There appears to be some difference of opinion between them as to their respective amusements; so they have come to a compromise. For every eighteen holes of golf played at least one cathedral must be visited, an agreement which, as he says, "preserves a delicate balance between the culture of the mind and of the body."

I do not know precisely how fond my correspondent is of cathedrals, but, presuming a temperate and reasonable affection for them, it seems to me that he has got all the worst of this bargain. A day's golf—yes, that might be fair enough, but to set a mere eighteen holes against a whole cathedral is iniquitous.

Just consider the two enterprises in light of their after-effects. A round of golf leaves a man comparatively fresh and unjaded, while a cathedral is more prostrating even than a picture gallery and makes of him a wreck, with aching legs and watering eyes.

I fancy my poor friend, after a whole day at Chester, dashing over to Hoylake, which he has never seen before, to be untimely ripped from it just when he is beginning to appreciate its flat and curious beauties. Or, again, here is a harder case—Canterbury and Sandwich! He plays a single round of St. George's and is not granted so much as to see the two other great courses which are next door to it. It is obvious that he has allowed himself to be scandalously over-reached.

I am writing to him to suggest a countermove. Let him go to Canterbury and behave in the most outwardly docile manner. Let him not only do the Cathedral thoroughly but also the ruins of St. Augustine's Monastery and St. Martin's Church; let him even throw out hints that Fordwich, with its delicious little town hall, should on no account be missed when they are so near to it. He may even add with an air of transparent innocence that it possesses a ducking stool for scolding wives. At the end of the day his family will be reduced to pulp. They will say, as did Mr. Micawber after a visit to Canterbury, that their ashes "will be found commingled in the cemetery attached to a venerable pile for which the spot has acquired a reputation, shall I say, from China to Peru."

At this moment he must unmask his bitterness, declaring that the bargain has not been kept. They have had much more than their pound of flesh. He must demand, at least, one round of Deal and one of Prince's in exchange for all that additional sightseeing, and they will be far too much exhausted to resist him. If he takes a firm stand, he may even get Rye and Littlestone thrown in and be let off Rochester altogether.

It will be seen that in a general way my sympathies are entirely with my friend. And yet at this particular moment I would personally rather see a cathedral than a golf course. Nor, I am convinced, am I alone in holding these sentiments. There was about last week-end's match at Sunningdale, in which various eminent persons were taking part, an air of lassitude. One of the most eminent persons even told me that the sight of a golf club filled him with horror and loathing. I was, to be sure, his partner, which may have had something to do with it.

Yet when it comes to quitting there are difficulties. When we arrive at this pass, the probability is that we have been playing badly, and that makes it for some of us harder, and not easier, to stop. We go on wondering what we were doing wrong; we are not satisfied with the knowledge that we were doing everything wrong because we were too tired of golf to do anything right. It is almost worthwhile to try just one more round in order that we may leave off in a more tranquil and reasonable frame of mind; but this may lead to an eternity of vain attempts.

If we can, like Mr. Bob Sawyer and Mr. Ben Allen, "try a little abstinence," we shall have a joyful day to which to look

167

forward. We may hardly have realized that we are convalescent when suddenly the desire to play golf again, the conviction that it is really quite a pleasant game, will burst upon us. We shall enjoy it as frantically as we do the whiting and milk-pudding—not in themselves an exciting diet—which are given us after another sort of illness.

By the time my American friend has finished his tour and come to London, his discipline somewhat relaxed, I hope I may have arrived at that happy state and be ready to play with him. So now give me a dim, restful, twilighty cathedral, or, failing that, a small chapel in a small corner of England.

Taylor and Braid

In this series of the champions of old times Harry Vardon had an article all to himself. The other two members of the Triumvirate, J. H. Taylor and James Braid, I will put together, partly because they come just, but still quite distinctly, below the incomparable Vardon, partly because they seem to me to make an entertainingly vivid contrast, the one to the other.

Taylor is an Englishman from Westward Ho! in Devon; Braid a Scotsman from Earlsferry in Fife. Braid was and is of all the great golfers perhaps the most calm, longheaded and philosophical; Taylor the most enthusiastic, bubbling and temperamental. Yet by some curious perversity Nature, which made Braid so calm made of him a slashing and dashing golfer while of Taylor the excitable she made just about the steadiest, safest, most accurate golfer that ever lived.

There could hardly be imagined in point of temperament two players more widely divergent, and yet they attained the same result in both being magnificent men in a pinch. Braid did it by endless patience, by accepting the rough with the smooth as being all in a day's work, by taking a cool detached view of his troubles and hoping for the best. Taylor did it by wrestling with himself and all the devils of golf in a kind of pent up white hot fever, emerging successful from the struggle and becoming, by dint of his conquest, a creature radiant and inspired.

You would imagine from those words that it was Taylor who had the more disastrous holes and recovered from them the more brilliantly, and Braid who kept more evenly on the tenor of his way with just now and then a stroke dropping and a four turning into a five. Yet by that strange perversity before mentioned, exactly the opposite was the case. Braid was and could not help being a slasher. Do not run away with the impression that he was a wild player. Of course he was not or he never could have come near to doing what the did, but he did lash at the ball as somebody described it, with a divine fury, that tremendous wrench round of his body, that right knee sinking almost to the ground at the finish as he gave the shot "just a little bit extra," that something more than a suspicion of the shut face, that habitual "draw" with which he played— all these things made for just a very occasional big hook that took his ball into very funny places. With his great strength and his great power of "sizing up" a situation he recovered from those places wonderfully, but still he did get into them and sometimes inevitably they cost him dear.

Taylor on the other hand had no vast length and did not attempt to gain it. He had not in his bag any terrific shot, any twenty or thirty additional yards up his sleeve to be produced at a crisis. What he had was the most peerless accuracy and a supreme command over the ball, especially when the wind roared and the rain came down in torrents, so that he pulled his cap still further down over his nose and set his jaw still more firmly. He had an enormous and well deserved reputation as a mashie (5 iron) player, but I think that in estimating the causes of his victory full justice was often not done to his wooden club play.

Within his limits—and if he was not long he was not short— Taylor was just about the best driver I ever saw with a beautifully true swing, rather flat and "round the corner" according to modern notions perhaps, but to my thinking a joy to watch. And how firm on his feet! As he struck the ball and more often than not when he had finished and come through, he was like a rock with his two feet planted on the ground as if they had taken root there. Possibly with a rather freer swing he might have got a little further for, though not tall, he was big and strong. But he was not to be tempted into any such experiments by the will o' the wisp of length. "Flat footed golf, sir, flat footed golf, there's nothing like it," I have often heard him exclaim with that formidable shake of the head which is so characteristic, and no man in the world can give greater emphasis to statements than can J. H.

Both were great iron players, Braid with a little more power of the two and an astonishing capacity for hitting with a cleek (2 iron), a club to which he has always remained faithful. I do not think there was anything to choose between them as regards results, but they differed in their methods of getting them. Taylor has always been a confirmed, almost an obstinate pitcher. It is one of his most cherished maxims that there are no hazards in the air, and, though of course he can play a running up shot well enough, he regards it as a "dirty scuffling shot." It used to be an old joke against him that he would insist upon pitching up to that deadly little seventeenth green at St. Andrews, perched between the devil of the bunker and the deep sea of the road, when even his skill could not make the ball stop there. The best of the joke was with him as he won two of his five championships at St. Andrews and his pitching has been his strongest asset. So if now and again he pitched away a stroke in deference to his great principle he could afford it.

Braid could pitch as well as need be, admirably well indeed, but his natural instinct was to play a running shot or a pitch-and-run when he could. No doubt his early training at St. Andrews where he went from his native Earlsferry to work as a joiner, had something to do with it; certainly there has been no greater master of this shot in all its forms. Being the more phlegmatic and having no principles on behalf of which to die, he was perhaps rather more open minded than Taylor and simply played the shot which he thought would pay him best at the time.

In the matter of putting Braid has had the more erratic and Taylor the steadier career. It used to be said of Taylor that he was the best two putts per green putter in the world. He varied very little; he was not a Willie Park or a Jack White; he did not overwhelm an enemy by the holing of long putts, but day in and day out he laid the approach putt near the hole and he popped the next one in. He was naturally a sound putter with a sound style and did not have to agonize over much, as I fancy, about his method.

171

Braid's case was just the opposite. When he first appeared he was a magnificent player up to the green and a pretty poor one when he got there. He missed far too many short putts. The long ones did not trouble him, but near the hole he was inclined to knuckle his right knee, move his body and push the ball out to the right of the hole. I remember many years ago having a day's golf with him when he described himself as putting "like an auld sweetie wife" and the description was just. However he thought and he practiced and he toiled and gradually he turned himself into a very good putter indeed.

He never looked entirely natural and at ease, his noticeably slow take-back of the club had a laborious air, he always had to take infinite pains, but handsome is as handsome does and for some years, when he was unquestionably at the top of the tree, his putting had much to do with his success. He taught himself by sheer determination to stand still and hit the ball truly.

Taylor won his first championship in 1894, Vardon in 1896. Braid, who is the same age, did not win his first until 1901. When once he had won he went on winning—in 1905, 1906, 1908 and 1910. Four times in six years was a great feat. During those years he was the dominating figure, and nobody holed more putts than he.

Well I could write about these two heroic figures forever, for not only are both great golfers, but each has as well at least some of the qualities of a great man. However, I must stop. I remember some years ago as I and a friend were just taking our candlesticks with many yawns to go to bed he propounded the problem: "Would you rather play golf like Braid or like Taylor?" We talked for another hour and came to no conclusion, nor will I give any answer to his question now. They occupy in golf twin pinnacles of exactly equal height.

Golf's Dread Disease

The other day I had staying in my house over the weekend a lady who had just begun to play golf. She had lately paid for a course of half a dozen lessons at a golf school and had undergone so far three of them. She had brought her bag of clubs with her and I suggested a little mashie (5 iron) play on the lawn. "Oh but," she exclaimed in a voice of terror, "I have not got so far as the mashie yet." She said it in the tone of a child who on being asked questions as to history lessons declares that it has only reached the Battle of Marathon and cannot deal with Julius Caesar or the Norman Conquest. After a little persuasion she put on her thickest boots, took her brand new virginal mashie and out we went.

The results, though painful to her and humiliating to me as an amateur teacher, were not uninstructive. With her first three shots she lofted the ball, as if to the manner born, straight down the lawn. Then without the least warning her fourth ball nearly decapitated me, who was standing a little to the right of her, and buried itself in shrubbery. "Heavens," she cried with a gasp, "what happened?"

I answered with reassuring words, but I said internally, "Ah! my poor lady, that has befallen you which befalls all of us sooner or later. You have socketed your first mashie shot." The disease, as the doctors say in their bulletins, "pursued its normal course." Another and yet another ball was hit from the same fatal part of the club-head. Here was my chance as a healer. I tried the orthodox cures upon her but they did not avail. Lastly in despair I handed her a club of my own having a twisted neck and no socket. Even that did not help her. Still the ball flew off at a violent tangent to the right till that shrubbery became a perfect gold mine of lost balls.

We both tried nobly and she had periods of comparative convalescence but when dusk began to fall the germ had not been wholly expelled. That which interested me, even while it made me feel ashamed and humbled was that, watch as

173

closely as I might, I could not see what it was that she was doing wrong, or why the ball was hit off the extreme heel. There is surely something about this dread disease of socketing which, as the reviewers say of a novel when they are hard put to it, "defies analysis." It comes mysteriously and it goes mysteriously, and it is far more utterly prostrating and incurable than any other golfing ailment.

I do not know how it is with other people but I have always had one golfing nighmare. I imagine myself having the simplest of pitches to play to the home hole, with several strokes in hand and the match humanly speaking won, and then the ball is hit off the socket into an unplayable spot in a bunker and the match is lost. It has never so far happened to me and only once has the horrid thought come to me when I actually had to play that crucial shot. That was in the semi-final of a tournament of some little importance; my adversay had been in fearful trouble; I had nothing to do but trundel the ball along in inglorius safety *but*—and it was a terrible but—on the right-hand side, just where a socketed ball would go, there was a drop into perdition, a terrible waste of sand and stones. How fervently did I thank Heaven at that moment that there was in my bag a mashie without a socket. Without it I firmly believe I should have been undone so overwhelming were my terrors. As it was I just knocked the ball along toward the green with some sort of indeterminate shot and all was well. Incidentally I won that tournament and I have never failed thankfully to carry that club round with me ever since.

Those who derive comfort from the misfortunes of others may relect with pleasure that socketing can attack as well the highest as the lowest. The words of the wise Sir Walter Simpson in the old Badminton book are still true. "When an adept's driving leaves him for a season," he wrote, "it does not do so entirely. His slicing, toeing, heeling are not so grossly manifest as at an earlier stage. It is otherwise with approaching. A medal winner unable to hit with any part except the socket of his iron is no uncommon phenomenon." Much greater men than mere medal winners can suffer. It is not I believe a libel to say that some years ago perhaps the best approacher in the world, J. H. Taylor, went through a period when he was scared out of his life by the thought of a socket. The advent of the horrid thing is moreover so sudden, as it was with my poor lady who did not know what had happened. It is like a thunderbolt out of a clear sky. I remember to have seen an admirable iron player, playing well and confidently in the semi-final of a championship, and then without any warning hitting three consecutive iron shots off the socket. Away went the ball each time to some unspeakable place, and away went all his chance of appearing in the final.

Much has been said and written about the cause and cure of this scourge. It is said to come from taking the club back too quickly, from using "too much right hand" or alternatively "too much wrist" from having the arms too free and unsupported by the body. All these things—one at one time and one at another—have no doubt something to do with it, but to know all this and more is not necessarily to be able to cure yourself. I have always thought that one of the best cures was that confided to me by the late Mr. Charles Hutchings, who won the championship when he was fifty-three years old and a grandfather, "Rip the club through with the right hand" was his formula. It was not, I suppose, orthodox, having regard to the doctrine of "Too much right hand," but I have known it to be very effective.

When all is said and done. I am inclined to think that the best cure is the simplest, namely a club without a socket. It may be inelegant, it may be a confession of weakness, but is it not wiser sometimes to run away than to fight? That poor lady to be sure did manage even to socket when there was no socket and that has shaken my faith a little. How she did it I did not know then and I do not know now, but she did. I only hope that golf school will be able to cure her for she lies heavy on my conscience.

Where to
Golf in Britain

I understand that I am tentatively to direct the footsteps of a
hypothetical American golfer among the golf courses of
the British Isles.

Something depends first of all on how he approaches our
shores. If he lands at Plymouth or Southampton, or if he goes
first to Paris and then flits across the Channel to Dover, he
will almost certainly and naturally rush straight to London.
But if he lands at Liverpool then I think he should stop there
for a day or two and see Hoylake and Formby, two admirable
seaside courses ready to his hand, of which Hoylake at any
rate is a classical one. Hoylake itself is a rather unprepossess-
ing suburb, and I am afraid my visitor may even not like the
course itself because it is superficially unattractive, being rather
flat and cut up by turf walls with the sand hills only as a background. Yet if he has faith and if there is a wind blowing, and
if he plays two rounds, I think he will realize something of its
real greatness. If he has anything of a pilgrim's soul in him he
ought to see it, because it is one of the homes of golf and the
home of three of the greatest amateur golfers that ever lived,
John Ball, Harold Hilton and Jack Graham.

Formby, I am quite sure he will like, although it is not so
good as Hoylake. Nevertheless, it has all the typically seaside
beauties, sand and bents and sand hills and lovely secret valleys in between in almost profligate abudance.

Both these courses and other good ones in the neighborhood such as Birkdale and Blundellsands, he can visit from
Liverpool, and now I will whisk him to London. However long
he likes to stay there he can play on a new and good course
every day—at least for a considerable time. London is lucky in
that within twenty or thirty miles of it to the south chiefly in
Surrey are big belts of sandy heathery fir tree country, such as
Pine Valley was made from, providing inland golf of the very

highest class. They are all easy to reach by train, but more easily and pleasantly reached by car. Sunningdale is an obvious place of pilgrimage, a lovely course and one, I find, that always appeals to American golfers. Then there is Walton Heath, home of the great James Braid who alone is worth a visit, a better course to my thinking than Sunningdale and an equally beautiful spot.

Woking possesses a trinity of fine courses, neighbors so close as almost to touch one another. Woking, West Hill and Worplesdon, St. George's Hill, Wentworth, Addington, Camberley Heath—I could write down more names of excellent heathery courses which can all be reached in a little under or a little over an hour's drive from London. And I will put in one park course, Stokes Poges, both because it is good and pretty and because it might fit in with a non-golfing pilgrimage to Windsor and Eton which are close by, and to the churchyard where Gray wrote his elegy.

Now supposing our visitor to be tired of London and to want a little more seaside golf where shall I send him? The west country is very engaging and Westward Ho! in Devonshire is a noble course as is Burnham in Somerset, but they are some way off whereas he can get to Sandwich in a couple of hours. He can stay at Sandwich itself which is peaceful or he can stay at Broadstairs or Ramsgate or Margate or Westgate if he wants a watering place of more life and cheerfulness and company. Moreover Sandwich provides three courses, the Royal St. Georges, Princes and Deal which is only a very little way off. I do not think that anywhere else are there three such fine courses so close together. Add them together, divide by three and get the average and the result will be hard to beat by any other one course in the world. It is the most typically seaside golf imaginable which is what I want my visitor to see, and set in a delightful piece of England. Sandwich itself, though golf has practically awakened it from its sleep, is still very peaceful, very drowsy, very twisty and narrow as to its streets, very old and bulgy as to its houses and in short a very engaging bit of old England.

THE HAPPY GOLFER

Once my friend—I feel I know him well enough to call him so—has got to Sandwich it would be a sin and a shame if he did not cross the border from Kent into Sussex and see another lovely old town and another fine golf course at Rye. There is no more beautiful old town in England than Rye (unless it be its neighbor, Winchelsen), standing with its red roofs huddled Flemish-fashion round its old church on the top of a cliff from which the sea has long receded. The golf, too, is of the very best and only a few miles off, across Romney Marsh, which is the country of Sheila Kaye Smith's novels, lies another good though not so good course, Littlestone. Incidentally Hastings (remember the famous battle?) is not far from Rye and would be a good place to stay whether for golf or sightseeing or both.

I feel I am treating the rest of England unkindly by dwelling so long on these Kent and Sussex courses but they are obvioiusly the right places for my friend to go. If he likes the east coast let him not miss Hunstanton and Brancaster in Norfolk. Pehaps he could go to them after going to Cambridge, supposing he wanted to see that seat of learning. There is plenty of good golf in Yorkshire and further north but nothing that cries aloud to be seen. I think it is time for him to take the train north to Scotland, as any pious pilgrim ultimately must.

Scotland has many courses but there is one at any rate that must be seen, St. Andrews, and three groups or clusters that ought to be seen, namely St. Andrews and its immediate neighbors, second, the cluster of East Lothian courses which may be called by the generic name of North Berwick, and third, the west coast courses which centre round Prestwick and Troon in Ayrshire.

If my friend is a general sightseer he may want to stop at Edinburgh where by the night train he will have arrived in good time for early breakfast. If this is so he need not bother his head about the inland courses round Edinburgh which are good but ordinary. Should he be purely a golfer he will push straight on to St. Andrews, have his breakfast on the train and arrive at the Mecca of all golfing pilgrims by about half-past nine. I am not going to describe St. Andrews to him but will merely warn him that (a) he must not mind if he does not always draw a time on the old course in the ballot, and (b) he must not be annoyed if he goes uncommonly slow. If he does not draw a time he must either get up very early in the morning to try to start before nine o'clock or else he must play on the new course or the Eden course which are both very good and have much of the right flavor or atmosphere, but are not, of course, the real thing.

As regards slowness of progress, he must just bear it. It is part of the entertainment. Let him derive consolation from this fact, that it makes no matter whether he has James Braid in front of him or an old lady who cannot drive fifty yards, the one will keep him back no more and no less than the other.

On Sunday there is no golf at St. Andrews and that is the day for him to drive over and play at Gleneagles. Here is a fine dramatic course in lovely hilly, almost highland scenery with the best hotel in Scotland. It is moreover a course with which, in my experience, American golfers always fall in love. If he can tear himself away for another day or two from St. Andrews he may go on to Carnoustie not far away in Forfarshire, a breeding place of great golfing families, such as the Simpsons and the Smiths and, incidentally, the home of Steward Maiden, on whose swing Bobby Jones is supposed to have founded his own.

North Berwick is only an hour or so from Edinburgh and provides greater choice of golf than any one place in the world. If St. Andrews is crowded North Berwick is more so and the round even slower with less compensation, nor do I personally find comfort in the fact that the crowd there is a fashionable one whose pictures are in the illustrated papers. It is an engaging course but a little of it goes a long way and after a day or so I suggest that my friend drive over to Gullane only a very few miles away. He can do this for several days in succession and play on a new course every day. Gullane has on one gorgeous stretch of turf three courses, two of them very good, with lovely views and to be played on by taking a ticket at a modest price.

THE HAPPY GOLFER

New Luftness, a private club course is on the same expanse of turf and only a short way off is Muirfield, on no account to be missed. This is a championship course—Jesse Sweetser won his championship there—and as fine and difficult a test of golf as need be. It is the private property of that ancient and illustrious body, the Honourable Company of Edinburgh Golfers (how noble a title!), and my friend must here get an invitation or a member to put his name down. This I am sure he will be able to do and then he can play the highest class of golf in comparative peace and quiet. There are other courses, too, such as Aberlady and Longniddry quite worth seeing and only a few miles further off.

If he goes to the west—and Ayrshire is an enchanting country—I propose to my friend that he should stay at Troon, which has plenty of accommodations. Here at his door are at least three good courses, that of the Troon Golf Club itself and two municipal ones as well, all truly seaside in character and with the loveliest of velvety turf. Then the next station to Troon is Prestwick and this he must not miss. Here too he must be careful to get an introduction. Having got it he can play in the utmost privacy on a classic course, in some ways the most fascinating of all, with tremendous hills and secret nooks and hollows and a rushing burn and the biggest of all cross-bunkers, the famous Cardinal. If I wanted to introduce a stranger who had never seen typical British seaside golf, Prestwick is one of the two places to which I should inevitably take him, Sandwich being the other. He might think this approach lucky or that tee shot blind but he must think the whole enchanting.

Now I really must stop. If my friend does half I have told him to he will in Allan Robertson's words have had a "Bellyful of gowf."

Who Was
Henry Vardon?

At Muirfield last May when the great body of onlookers
went surging after the victorious Hagen, there were a
few, liking art for art's sake, apart from victory, and disliking a
crowd, who went elsewhere. This little band of connoisseurs,
at once so modest and so select, was to be seen following
Macdonald Smith and Harry Vardon. The one might well have
won, but had had a bad time and was out of the hunt; the
other born in 1870, could not hope to win at this time of day.
So they were to be watched purely because they were two of
the most graceful and beautiful of all golfers.

Till they got to the greens there was nothing in it between
them; the older man was fully holding his own in the power of
his long game, in the crispness and accuracy of his iron shots.
Only when it came to the putting, Vardon's old enemy beset
him; he moved his body, he stabbed at the short ones, he went
off "at half cock." Otherwise the years might have rolled away
and here was still a great master and we might almost have
been looking at the invincible player who had dominated golf
at the beginning of the century.

I am not going to argue as to whether or not Vardon is the
greatest golfer that ever lived. These comparisons are futile.
It is enough that he was the golfer of his time. He won the
British Open championship in 1896, 1898, 1899, 1903,
1911 and 1914; he won the American championship in 1900.
He was probably at his very best in 1889 and 1899 before his
visit to America. In point of health and strength he was not
quite the same man afterwards, and he himself has said
that he thinks he left a little of his game there. It was not
till some little time later this his actual and very serious
illness developed, and he won two more championships after
he was well again, but never again did he show the same ut-

terly crushing superiority, which caused Andrew Kirkaldy to say that he would break the heart of an iron ox.

Of the "triumvirate"—Vardon, Braid and Taylor—Taylor is actually the youngest by a few months, but he was the first to make his name. He leaped into fame in 1893 when he began knocking down the big men like ninepins and in both 1894 and 1895 he was champion. Very few people had heard of Harry Vardon then, nobody perhaps save a few golfers in the north of England who had backed him in a home-to-home match against Sandy Herd and seen him badly beaten. In the winter of 1895-96 half a dozen leading professionals were asked to go out to play at Pau; someone of discerning judgment made Vardon one of the party and the rest of the world asked "who is this fellow Vardon?"

Then in the spring of 1896 Taylor, twice the champion, played Vardon on his home course at Ganton in Yorkshire and came away beaten by a pocketful of holes and declared that here was the man that he feared most in the coming championship. It was a sound piece of prophecy for the two tied at Muirfield and Vardon won on playing off. In the next year the new star waned a little and then in 1898 blazed out in full glory.

For the next two years, if Vardon was in the field no one looked any further for the winner; he crushed everyone. He once beat Taylor at Newcastle in Ireland by 12 and 11 and Taylor was playing his game. In 1900 he went to America and after that he was, right up till the war, one of the two or three unquestioned best, but he was never again, as he had been, in a completely different class from all the other golfers.

I remember very well the first time I saw him play. It was in the late summer of 1896 and he had won his first championship in the spring. I went over to Ganton, where he was then professional, for a day's golf and there by good luck was the great man driving off. He hit just the sort of drive that he always did—dead straight and rather high, the ball seeming to float with a particularly lazy flight through the air. The shot was obviously a perfect one and yet I was not quite so much impressed as I had expected to be. The style was so different from what I had been taught to admire; the club seemed to be taken up in so outrageously upright a manner, with something of a lift.

No doubt I was stupid and uneducated. So at least were other people who ought to have known much better than I, and the general impression at first could be summed up in the learned Mr. Edward's words, "These Vardons are not pretty players." Moreover I think his style did change a little and become both more elegant and more sound. At any rate one of his most distinguished contemporaries has told me so, adding that when Vardon first appeared be used to let his right elbow fly out a little at the top of his swing and he certainly never did that afterwards. However that may be, all the world soon became converted and by 1898 his swing was recognized not only as one of genius but also as one of surpassing ease and grace.

Well now, what were the characteristics both of his method and its results which made him so devastating a conqueror? Results are easier to tackle and I will take them first. Vardon was first of all a magnificent driver. He was with a gutty ball uncommonly long, especially down wind, and he was very straight. Taylor had been regarded as inhumanly accurate and so he was. Now here came Vardon who rivalled his accuracy and added to it a little something more of freedom and power. He had a gift of hitting long carrying shots and, because of his upright swing, the ball would sit down with but little run where it pitched. This gift was of enormous value through the green. The brassie (2 wood) was not atrophied then, there were lots of wooden club shots to be played up to the pin and Vardon, who often played them with his driver, could and did put the ball nearer the hole than other men could with their mashies (5 iron). It was his most overpowering stroke and, even if he had been a bad putter then (which he was not), it left him little putting to do.

183

Then he was superb with all iron clubs. He could command great length, if he needed it, and had in particular at one time a driving mashie (1 iron) which was as a driver in his hand. He was beautifully accurate in all pitching shots. Taylor had got there first and acquired the reputation of the greatest mashie player in the world, but I think Vardon was just as good. He was a good approach putter and at any rate an adequate holer out, though without the touch and delicacy of the really outstanding putter.

He had a calm and cheerful temperament, the game seemed to take very little out of him and he could fight, if need be, without appearing to be fighting at all. All these very valuable qualities, but, if one thing is to be picked out that made him supreme, it was that unique power of hitting long soaring wooden club shots up to the hole side. "Two-shot" holes could be worthy of their name then, and given a course that had a number of them, Vardon was invincible. Other men might be scrambling onto the verge of the green and getting a certain number of fours, but he was putting for threes.

As to his style, photographs of him are probably familiar to the reader and give at any rate some impression. One thing noticeable in those pictures is that by comparison with the modern school Vardon certainly made no fetish of the stiff left arm. Another thing is the uniform beauty of the follow-through. Time after time he would come right through, drawn to his full height, the club right round over his left shoulder, the hands well up, the left elbow tolerably high. It was the ideal copy-book follow-through and he did it every time with an almost monotonous perfection.

Neither photograph, however—the top of the swing nor the finish of it—gives any real notion of how he took the club up and his method is very unlike anybody else's. First of all he was a conspicuous example of the doctrine of "hands leading." In his day the books used to tell us that the head of the club should go back first and the wrists begin at once to turn away. In fact I do not believe that any of the good players did anything of that kind, but they thought and taught that they did and the human eye was not quick enough to detect the fallacy. In Vardon's case, however, it was clear that he did none of these things; one could actually see the hands leading and the club head going back for some distance in a straight line before he slung it to the top of the swing. Neither does any photograph convey the small but still perceptible touch of lift in the upswing nor the little touch of sway.

His was essentially an upright swing in the days when orthodox swings were flat and was the more noticeable accordingly. He took the club up very straight, "too straight" as any self-respecting caddie would have said in instructing his master. Then by way of natural compensation he flung the club head well out behind him and brought it down onto the ball with a big sweep. It was a beautifully free movement of one having a natural gift for opening his shoulders and hitting clean. And, of course, like the movements of all really great golfers, it was instinct with that mysterious thing called rhythm. No golfer in the world, not even Bobby himself, was ever more perfectly rhythmic than Harry Vardon.

I am letting my enthusiasm run me into too many pages and must pull up. One of the most notable features of Vardon's iron play was its beautiful cleanness. He just shaved the roots of the grass and made no gaping wounds in the turf, and that was so, even in the shot singularly ill-named the "push-shot," about which industrious journalists wrote columns when Vardon was devastating the country. Down came the club hitting the ball first and going on to graze the turf, and away flew the ball starting low and then rising gradually to fall very dead from the undercut put on it. He played this shot often with a cleek (2 iron) and he played it with his mid-iron; he had not a whole series of irons to play it with as his successors have today.

In re-reading what I have written I find I have said nothing about the Vardon grip. Well Vardon certainly discovered it for himself and made it popular; but Taylor at Westward Ho!

had also discovered it for himself while Vardon was doing the same in Jersey, and Mr. Laidlay had discovered it long before either of them at North Berwick, while those two were tiny boys. Still it is a convenient name and I hope the day will never come when some young golfer who has just learned it asks "Who was Vardon?"

1930

Hard Times

The argument which once used to rage as to whether or not golf has improved seems of late to have died down. Perhaps the old gentlemen who upheld the old heroes have died too. At any rate comparisons are odious and rather futile. It must surely be that with thousands of golfers where once there were ten the play is better and with that I will cautiously leave it. I don't want to argue or compare but now and then there do come to us amusing glimpses into the dim past which for a moment make one want to do so.

The other day I chanced to mention in an article the great foursome (alternate shots) played over three greens in 1849—Allan Roberton and Tom Morris against the two Dunns. This brought me a letter from a gentleman at St. Andrews who is hard on ninety years old. In looking through some family papers he had found a letter from an uncle of his written to a brother in India giving the scores of the match at St. Andrews. He kindly sent me a copy of it and it thrilled me to the marrow. Even to my American readers who do not know St. Andrews—and most of course do not—I think the scores will be illuminating and so I set them down:

First round
Allan and Tom
Out — 6 5 6 5 5 5 5 4 4 — 45
Home — 6 4 5 5 7 7 4 6 6 — 50
95

The Dunns
Out — 6 5 4 6 6 6 4 4 5 — 46
Home — 5 3 5 6 5 5 5 6 6 — 46
92

Second Round
Allan and Tom
Out — 5 5 7 5 6 4 6 3 5 — 46
Home — 3 4 5 5 6 5 5

BERNARD DARWIN

The Dunns
Out — 6 6 5 5 8 5 4 4 4 — 47
Home — 4 4 4 5 8 5 5

Allan and Tom won by three up and two to play.

For those who do not know the course I may just add that the two short holes are the eighth and eleventh and that the two long ones the fifth and fourteenth, that the par of the course today is 72 and that the only hole played by either side under par was the three which Allan and Tom did at the tenth.

Bear in mind that here were the four unquestionably great players of the day and they were taking well over ninety to get round a course which as regards the position of the greens was much what it is today, from shorter tees. Yet what an utterly different course, infinitely narrower with gorse creeping in on the player in places which are now perfect fairway, with all manner of bad lies, with greens which were known for their different evil qualities—one for roughness, the next for sandiness, the one for its dense covering of heather roots. The holes were probably too big, unless indeed, they were freshly cut for the match, since in those days there were no tins and the holes grew bigger as hand after hand dived into them for a pinch of sand to tee the balls. That big hole was the only conceivable advantage those old heroes had, and they had to get a feather ball into it and not a very round one. The gutty had just come in at the time of the match, but it is certain that Allan Robertson would not have played with it, for it was on this rock that Allan and Tom split a few months earlier.

I can sit and pore over that score and try to imagine how it was done—how in the name of goodness did they halve the last hole in six? At that hole, once the burn right in front of the tee is crossed, there is nothing in the way. A drive and a pitch and run is all that is wanted. Mighty hitters have driven the green with a wind behind and ordinary mortals can get into the hollow short of it. How did those champions take six? I suppose there was a strong wind against them in which case they could not nearly get home in two. Perhaps they needed three full shots; perhaps they took three putts apiece. I wish I could see it.

As to the two eights that the Dunns took at the two long holes no doubt the gorse has something to say to that, and I am sure there must have been a fierce wind for it is to be remembered that Allan once holed St. Andrews in 79 and that is a very different thing from 92, isn't it? The fives doubtless represented good play, for, with a gutty, most of the St. Andrews holes needed two wooden club shots, and with a feather ball they must have needed two and a bit. It is all terribly difficult to imagine.

Golf must have been an exciting game to watch with the best of players taking sixes and sevens. That is what we must always remember—the character of the lies for indeed even I can remember the time when one remarked "I've got a good lie," where today one only comments on a bad lie.

In a contemporary account of the final installment of this match at North Berwick there is a passage which throws a bright light: "Each side has its band of supporters. Those of the Musselburgh men (The Dunns) however, owing to the nearness of the links to North Berwick, preponderated, and they were led by Gourlay, the well known ball maker. So great was the ferment and anxiety to see whose ball had the better lie, that, no sooner were the shots played, than off the whole crowd ran helter-skelter, and as one or the other lay best so demonstrations were made by each party." It would be sound discipline for us today if we had to feel ourselves lucky to get a good lie. It would make us understand the sixes and sympathize with the eights.

I feel I ought to apologize for this antiquarian excursion. Snow is lying outside my window as I write, which makes golf impossible. That must be my excuse, and besides I do think it rather interesting. It is good for us now and them to visualize the difficulties those old warriors had to meet—the bad greens and lies and the seas of gorse and the lighter balls that were so easily blown away into them. "Its aye fechtin' against ye" said

Allan and indeed the game was fighting against them harder than it does against us with everything made so smooth—billiard tables to putt on and steel shafts to prevent us going as crooked as we deserve. Those scores have made me feel not arrogant but humble and it is in a humble spirit that I write.

The Third Leg of the Grand Slam

The American Open championship was played during one of our very busiest sporting weeks in England. There was the Oxford-Cambridge cricket match and that between Eton and Harrow following one another at Lords; then on the last two days at Leeds the third match between England and Australia began and we stood spellbound before the astonishing batting of Don Bradman, the young Australian prodigy who in the ruthlessness and consistency of his scoring promises to be the Bobby Jones of cricket. There was also the athletic meeting between Princeton and Cornell, Oxford and Cambridge. So, you see, we had plenty to distract our attention, and yet a great many of us had time to think about Interlachen, to wonder what was happening there, to picture to ourselves the blazing sunshine, the shirt-sleeved players and the spectators under umbrellas, and when we came down for breakfast we made a dash for one particular corner of our morning paper.

Of course, we all wanted Bobby to win yet again. There could be no possible doubt about that. With all respect to many other good fellows and good golfers, there was only one favorite in this country. Our Friday morning's paper left us in a very good humor for our man had done a 71, tremendously good and yet not too alarmingly so. It left Bobby just where we thought he would like to be, namely at the top of the tree but not actually on the topmost branch of all. We thought that he would do better, to use the language of running, if he were hanging at the shoulder of the leader rather than making the pace himself. We remembered that when he won our Open championship at St. Andrews in 1927 he had said that "the strain of being in the lead was awful."

Armour and Macdonald Smith were ahead of him by just one stroke and both are great golfers but somehow we did not think they would stay ahead all the time. There is no lovelier golf player in the world than Macdonald Smith, and he seems to be able to win everything but a championship. At Hoylake he had thrown away his chance with his second round, and then, when there was practically no chance left, had come with a wonderful spurt in the last round and done a 71 when a 69 was needed. It is sometimes easier for a player of a certain temperament to play brilliantly when there is no hope than to play steadily when there is great hope. Personally I was much more afraid on Bobby's behalf of Horton Smith who was just behind him with a 72.

So much for Friday morning's paper. Saturday's was equally cheerful for it told us that Bobby was at the top with 71 and 73. There was no mention of Horton Smith and that was odd. At any rate Bobby was leading, and then came the early editions of the evening papers telling us that Horton Smith had done a 70 and was leading the field by two shots. I must admit that at that point my faith in Bobby came near to faltering a little. Horton Smith is a golfer that impresses me enormously; his great hour is bound to come soon, and I wondered whether it had now struck. I heartened myself by saying what I had said on the first day, that Bobby is better when coming up from behind, that it is just as well for him not to lead and so on, but still I confess to have had too little faith and to have felt distinctly uneasy as I went to bed on Saturday night and wondered whether it was all over by that time.

Breakfast is always late on a Sunday, but I was up betimes, while the table was still being laid. The Sunday paper was not in the dining room and I inquired fiercely why the ____! it had not come. I must have been terrifying for it made its appearance from the back regions is less than no time. I tore it open and there was the news, though I had to look on two different pages for it. One page only told me of that overwhelming 68, which seemed to make things sure; the other announced in the baldest telegraphic language that he had won. After that, breakfast seemed very good indeed, and I could wait with a placidity bordering on indifference for further details on Monday. When they came they made me feel in one respect something of a true prophet for Macdonald Smith had made, as he had at Hoylake, a splendid forlorn hope of a spurt which only just failed and yet was almost bound to.

Well, there it is. Bobby has won and now wants only one more victory at Merion to set up such a record as no other man can ever hope to equal. In that matter he may be said to have done that already, but one more win would make it yet more complete and more entirely impregnable. I don't know whether other people can find anything striking or original to say about it, but I cannot. Only just this morning I chanced to meet J. H. Taylor and made the obvious opening remark "So Bobby has done it again." J. H. has as a rule a fine flow of words but he, too, was speechless. "Wonderful, sir, wonderful" was all he could say and then two or three times over "I can't understand it." He went on to say he could understand any man having a great year, then staying quiet for a little while and then having another, but what was so incredible was that Bobby could keep on doing it year after year and all the time.

The only thing I could think of saying—and Heaven knows it was dull and pedestrian enough—was that of the few unquestionably great golfers in history Bobby was the best putter, that others such as J. H. himself had good and bad days on the green, but that Bobby had no bad putting days, and that his best days were much better than theirs. How many titles would Vardon have won had he been able to putt like Bobby? As many as Bobby perhaps.

The Story of A and B

"You just come away," said Mr. Weller, seizing his master by the arm and dragging him out of the office in Freeman's Court. "Battledore and shuttlecock's a wery good game, when you an't the shuttlecock and two lawyers the battledores, in which case it gets too excitin' to be pleasant."

This piece of wisdom at once occurred to me when I opened a letter the other day and found two golfers of a legal turn of mind asking me to settle a dispute between them. However, I was somewhat reassured on reading farther. It seemed that they were not really so very angry with one another. They reminded me of Tweedledum and Tweedledee, who said, "Let's fight till 6 and then have dinner." Indeed, at one time I came almost to entertain a suspicion that they had concocted this dispute with a view to doing what is, I believe, known in vulgar language as pulling my leg. Here, at any rate, are the facts as told to me, on which anyone can form as a good a judgment as I can. For those who do not take golfing law too seriously they are not devoid of humour.

The two people concerned are A and B, each a golfer of some ten month's standing, and each bursting with a natural and proper ambition to go round in under a hundred. There is a third person mentioned, one C, but I really do not know what it has to do with him. He dwells on a lofty pinnacle, for he has a handicap of 15, and he appears to have fomented the quarrel to the best of his powers.

A little while ago A and B went out—and here I had better quote exactly from the case stated for my opinion—"for a day's golf, intent on breaking 100." It will be observed that nothing is said of their playing a match, and this point will hereafter appear to be of some possible importance. At the first hole there is a hedge bounding the course on the right, and if I am accurate in my guess I have often sliced into it myself. At any rate, A did so off the first tee, and, according to a local rule, he should have taken the ball out of the hedge and dropped it within one club's length under penalty of one stroke. What he did was to say, "I am going to have another," and have it he did. As he walked towards his second ball he added in a firm tone, "I am not going to count that first one." Thereupon B, whom I should judge to be by comparison a mild-mannered man, ventured to protest. What A said I do not know, but the hole was played out *pendente lite*, and they continued the round, possibly in moody silence. At the end, A's score, exclusive of that first drive, was 99. He had achieved his heart's desire, but it may be that B's tendency to sniff, and the perfunctory nature of his congratulations, rather took the gilt off the gingerbread. B's score is not recorded; he remains at this point in the background of the story, a silent, disapproving figure.

As the two walked away from the last green they met C, and then the argument began in earnest. A said that after his first drive he had abandoned that round and had begun another one. B and C retorted with a *reductio ad absurdum*; he might stand there and drive balls until he drove one three hundred yards. A said certainly, of course he might, provided that after each unsatisfactory drive he announced that he was about to begin a new round; further, that in this particular case he had abandoned his first round purely as a matter of personal convenience and that—mark this!—"he was not even having a match with B." I regret to add that later on he became so far personal and acrimonious in his tone as to insinuate that B was jealous of him because he had broken one hundred, and so passed into a higher class. I think he must have received some provocation from B and C before he sank to this. The two allies now tried to soothe him by saying that it was very hard luck to have the cup dashed from his lips just by one hedge but—they stuck to their point.

> *And now they never meet in grove or green*
> *By fountain clear or spangled starlight sheen,*
>   *But they do square—*

to the discomfort of all concerned.

They begin with the greatest friendliness, they talk about Plato or the new French Premier (they do sound alarmingly "high-brow"), but they always come back to the sore point. And so that is why I am called upon to play the part of the poor innocent shuttlecock.

I have only once heard before of a similar case. There was a golfer I used to know who made a habit of going on to the first tee and hitting off ball after ball until he had thoroughly satisfied himself. Then he started his round with the chosen ball, and his caddie cleared up the snowstorm in miniature which had descended on the first fairway. There was much less excuse for him than for A, for he was a scratch player; and, what is more, he had the really magnificent audacity to start thus on monthly medal days. I do not know that he entered into any fine shades of argument as to abandoning the round; he just did it, and his fellows affectionately submitted to it as one of his little ways.

I really cannot regard that most singular golfer as constituting a precedent, and so what am I to say to these disputants? It is open to me to take the high line, to tell A not to think so much about his score, but to play a proper match as a Christian golfer should. I might quote to him Sir Robert Hay, who, when asked his scored, replied that he could only answer that question on two days of the year, the Spring and Autumn medal days. I shall not do that, however, for I always feel that Sir Robert snubbed his admirer in too fierce and Johnsonian a manner, and A, as an ambitious young player, needs not snubs but encouragement. Moreover, if he likes to say that he did go round in 99, he seems to have a certain ridiculous measure of right on his side.

I remember many years ago an Open Champion, one of the greatest that ever lived, starting out on a round with an amateur. Both got into trouble at the first hole, whereupon the champion said, "let's go back and begin again," and so they did. I fancy the champion went round in 69 or so after that and nobody raised any churlish objections. Shall there be one law for the rich and another for the poor, one for that most illustrious of golfers and another for the struggling, hopeful A?

It seems to me eminently a case for settlement out of court. Let me suggest that A and B once more set out together for a day's golf, but not in the morning; let them have a very good lunch first, and let them play a match, deeming their scores only of a secondary importance. Each will be in a mood so bland and replete that he will turn a tolerably blind eye to the other's "approximations." At the end each will declare that he has done a 98; they will live happily ever after, and if C likes to turn up a sceptical nose, well, let him!

A Case of Short Putt-Itis

L ast month there was played one of the pleasantest and
most interesting of all our English tournaments, which produces each year an ever larger entry, namely the Mixed Foursomes at Worplesdon. It was won by a very strong couple,
Miss Molly Gourlay, who is at the moment champion both of
England and France, and Major Hezlet who is champion of
Ireland and has played in several Walker Cup matches. They
had two terrific struggles which only ended beyond the last
green. Against Miss Wethered and her partner, Colonel
Hamilton, they won at the twentieth hole, where Miss
Wethered having played amazingly and heroically, even for
her, showed how bitterly ironic a game of golf can be by missing a four-foot putt to keep the game alive. In the final, played
in torrents of rain, they had to go to the thirty-ninth hole
before beating Miss Joy Winn and Mr. Longstaffe, whose last
two putts simply refused to move on a saturated quagmire of a
green.

I only give so much history to lead up to my point, which is
that the winners would never have been so hard pressed and
would indeed have won comfortably, if poor Major Hezlet had
not been afflicted with the worst attack of short-putt-itis that
I ever saw. We have all had days of missing short putts—dreadful days of it, more dreadful as we believe than anything else
that could possibly happen to us but, on my word of honor, I
can say that in all my watching, I never saw such a bad one as
this was. It was like going to see a man hanged or suddenly
seeing somebody fall down in a fit; one felt an overpowering
impulse to turn away the eyes from too painful a spectacle.

Here was a very fine golfer playing up to the green very fine
golf, but when he was a yard from the hole—and of course by
the malevolence of the golfing fates he always *was* a yard from
the hole—he could not as much as hit the edge of it with his

putt. He could not force himself to take the club back from the ball and he could not make himself hit the ball. Yet he is by nature quite a good putter. It was an attack of putt paralysis—a complete inability to do something which any old lady who had never seen golf before could have done with ease and the handle of her umbrella. No golfing physician could have been of any service. It was a clean case for a hypnotist.

I would not intrude on the reader my own humble and obscure complaints, but for the fact that I often suffer from a rare form of short-putt-itis which is the exact converse of the one I have been describing. I have pictured a poor wretch who could not take his putter back. My disease is that on certain black days I cannot stop it from going back. Here I am at four feet from the hole, and all that the ball wants is the gentlest of little hits, and yet my absurd club head goes back and back and still further back, nearly as far as the length of the putt, and I *can't* stop it. It is as if I were employing a sixteen-pound hammer to drive in a small nail, and, what I must look like to any spectator, I shudder to think. The end is easily pretold; when at last my club consents to stop my body gives a fearful lurch forward and the head of the club either hits the ball twice as far as I intended or barely reaches it at all.

I wonder if anybody else has had this disease? I suppose no golfing ailment is unique. If there is another victim I wish he would tell me how he cured himself. My natural method is to take the putter back very slowly and rather far, and I have exaggerated it so as to lose all rhythm. Similarly Major Hezlet's natural method is to take the club back rather shortly and sharply and he had temporarily exaggerated that. But in both cases a golfing ailment can become a purely neurasthenic one and the victim wants somebody who will put him to sleep by mystic passes and tell him quite simply not to be a fool.

A Rule Is a Rule
Is a Rule

On a day in March eighty-seven years ago the members of the Royal Blackheath Golf Club assembled to play for their medal, and here is the record of it in their minutes. "This day a strong muster assembled to play for the medal. The weather was extremely favourable. *The hazards beautifully interesting from fulness of all of water."*

The italics are mine, because the sentiments there expressed are so very different from ours today. Even those heroic old Scotsmen, I suspect found the hazards just a little too interesting because the winner, the Hon. Fox Maule, took 173 strokes to do twenty-one holes, and a certain Mr. Black Tertius took just ninety-nine more, 272. Still perhaps the feeling of having nobly endured and stuck to the rigour of the game may have consoled them.

By comparison with them, most of us are, I fear, degenerate and the two captains of Oxford and Cambridge have just been creating a storm in a teacup or rather in a cup of casual water. They tried from the best of motives to improve on the Rules of Golf. I am afraid their experiment was rather a failure. The match was played at Hoylake; the course had suffered from heavy rain and snow and most of the bunkers were full of water. Casual water in bunkers does make for what we call "bad luck," especially when we ourselves are the victims of it and so the two young captains tried to make a more equitable rule. To be precise, they made three. They allowed a player to drop in a dry spot in the bunker, if he could find one. They let him treat certain bunkers as out of bounds and play another shot under penalty of loss of distance. They let him treat bunkers round about the green virtually as if they were not bunkers at all and drop behind them without any penalty.

As far as I saw, this new and complex code did not in any way affect the result of the match which, by the way, Oxford won easily, but neither did it help to remove "unfairness" or alleviate "bad luck." It went against one's golfing instincts to see players going into bunkers, often with thoroughly bad shots, and then picking out not a penny the worse. It was, no doubt, a great mistake not to abide by the rules of the game in an important match of this sort. I do not personally feel so violently about it as do some people who write about "prostituting the game" and so on. I felt at the time much more inclined to laugh at them than either to cry over or swear at them, but I do wish they had not done it. Rules are rules and when once we, who are doubtless very discreet, begin to change them there is no knowing to what ridiculous lengths indiscreet persons may go.

I do not think that in all the pother and correspondence that has ensued anybody has mentioned the old Blackheath precedent, which is indeed rather musty by this time, but people did quote very freely the famous water shot out of the Alps bunker played by Freddie Tait against John Ball in 1899. "What was good enough for the great men" they said at some length, but that was hardly fair because that match was played with the gutty ball which floated and the modern ball sinks. However one instance of a great water shot with the rubber-core ball has been cited in an article by Mr. Croome in the *Morning Post*, and I think it is so interesting I am going to steal some of it here.

The hero of the story is Mr. John Ball, and it happened in the last championship but one before the war. "John Ball was two down going to the fifteenth and had put his second into Johnnie Low's bunker just short of the green, where it lay covered with water. Before the players came up, I stuck a club into the water which wetted the shaft over more than the breadth of my hand. My neighbor in the gallery was a Hoylaker, and I remember expressing to him my opinion that John was done for. 'You can never say that about John Ball,' he replied. but I doubt if he or anyone else expected to see John wade into the water and hit his ball three or four yards past the pin.—Later I was told, not by the Master himself but by one of his admirers, who claimed to be passing on the explanation at second hand, how the feat is performed. You take an iron with not too much loft on it and swing so that the blade cuts into the water as a knife blade slices cheese. The club head reaches the ball while the waters are still divided and nicks it out before they have had time to close again. The explanation sounds plausible, but in all probability, Mr. John Ball is the only man who can say whether it really accords with the facts."

That stroke is interesting as a *coup-de-maître*, but I do not think it should induce the less talented of us to do anything but humbly pick out and drop when we are in a watery bunker. Incidentally much of the water in the Hoylake bunkers was a great deal deeper than four inches, it was often a foot or more and no genius could have got the ball out. There was nothing for it but to lift. The pity is that the lifting was not done under the proper penalty.

Mr. D. Wallace of Balgrummo

It is a little curious that at the present moment the golfers who are not so young as they were, and might be expected to be growing more drowsy in their progress round the links, are complaining of the dilatory habits of the younger generation. So far as I can judge, we are right, and yet there are one or two remarks that perhaps ought to be made.

One is that in the nature of things we should be sure to be complaining of something; if we did not think they went too slow we should think they went too fast. The other is that while we reprobate the mote in our young brother's eye, as he lies on his stomach, squinting along the line of his putt, we forget the beam, not in our own eyes of course, but in those of some of our contemporaries. *Vixere fortes*, &c., and we can all remember players who would have yielded the palm for leisureliness to no golfer now breathing.

The different generations have probably railed against each other in the matter of pace since golf began, and a kind friend has just supplied me with a very pleasant piece of evidence to that effect. This is an extract from the *Fife Herald* of 1858 describing some of the play in the famous tournament at St. Andrews in that year. Romantically minded golfers who delve in old books need not be told that this tournament was won by that then famous player, Mr. Robert Chambers, and I think that Mr. C. E. S. Chambers wrote some little account of it not many years ago. The particular match described in my extract was in the sixth round between Mr. D. Wallace of Balgrummo and Mr. Patrick Alexander, the one representing the "exceeding caution and extreme method" of the old school, the other the "brilliant driving and rapid play" of the new. "Philosophical spectators," we are told, were anxious to observe what the effect of Mr. Wallace's methods would be, and here is the most engaging description of them:—

204

"Stout Balgrummo is of good porte, with a slight stoop (from long practice in putting), and makes his appearance on the links arrayed in the orthodox scarlet, with a nondescript cap drawn over the back of his head. He takes a serious interest in the match in hand and knows better than to smile or fritter away his energies in vain babbling to surrounding friends. But chief of all the salient points of the antique school, Mr. Wallace possesses the gift of coolness in an eminent degree. He is not the man to rush frantically to his ball and hit it in a confused manner . . . . Balgrummo lies some six or eight club lengths from the hole; it is required that he do play his putt. This is a complicated business with Mr. Wallace. First of all, he takes his putter and carefully smooths the proposed pathway to the hole. Secondly, he squats behind the ball and eyes the line of his put for a few minutes. Then sedately walking to the rear of the hole he compares that point of sight with the other. Of a sudden he perceives a refractory twig of grass sticking up mid-way, and rising solemnly from behind the ball he walks forward and carefully bends down the delinquent verdure. After all which he prepares to play, and 10 to 1 the shot puts the best of the hole to his credit."

That last sentence is a little mysterious, but at any rate Mr. Wallace put the best part of more holes to his credit than did his adversary. He ought to have won at the Corner of the Dyke, but only halved the hole through "over-caution in putting." He did, however, win at the Burn by three and one. "Our space," the reporter goes on, "precludes the intention of further analysing the cause of Mr. Alexander losing this match, and we believe we have pretty fully explained the reason already." I think he had, for the indelible impression left on my mind is that long before he got to the Corner of the Dyke, Mr. Alexander wanted to murder Mr. Wallace, and that the *Fife Herald*, having the law of libel before its eyes, did not like to say so.

Some of Balgrummo's proceedings would today be open to question. That habit of making a pathway to the hole was, I know, a recognized one, but I have my doubts about bending the "delinquent verdure." That is, by the way, a delightful phrase which I propose to add to a long since exhausted vocabulary. But did Balgrummo really do it? Perhaps he did, and no doubt those learned persons who know all about the Aberdeen code of 1783 could tell me whether he was allowed to; but really they are so oppressively learned, when they once begin, that I rather hope they won't.

To have played against Balgrummo must have been a shattering experience, but merely to read about him is so agreeable that I cannot help feeling a little sad because he did not win the final. However, he got the second prize, "a beautiful set of clubs, the work of M'Ewan, Musselburgh, and a dozen Gourlays of different weights, all enclosed in a handsome box with silver plate." So he had not wasted all those minutes during which he had squatted behind his ball, and no doubt he exhibited a sturdy contempt for the jibes and sneers of the exasperated young slashers. I wonder if he played as slowly as— well, as Mr. X and Mr. Y do now.

1931

The Putter

For any one who has a feeling for the old things of golf, a peculiar romance hangs round the name of Hugh Philp. He may, I take it (though I am not learned in music), be called the Stradivarius of club makers. At any rate, he was the first man, whose name is known to us, to turn clubmaking into a fine art. Before he came, clubs had been thick, clumsy and loutish. He made them elegant and tapering, and full of graceful curves. There are still a good many in existence in the possession of hereditary golfers or lucky collectors, but I never had one or dreamed of doing so, and now suddenly I have become the possessor of a Philp putter, and that in a fittingly romantic manner.

A gentleman whom I have never met, though I remember his name from old golfing days, has sent me a letter "out of the blue." He says that he is now too old to use his faithful Philp any more, and since he believes me to have a proper veneration for such things, he has generously offered to give it to me. Could a more delightful surprise befall any golfer? It may be imagined with what gratitude I wrote my acceptance, and with what eager footsteps I ran with it to the post office.

Not only was this putter made by Philp, but its pedigree has even this further interest: that the club was used by a famous old golfer, Bob Kirk. Bob Kirk used to play matches with Young Tommy Morris, and David Strath and the other great ones of the 1860s and 1870s, and it was a chance remark of mine about him in an article (he once won a big match by playing a lefthand shot) that put the notion into my benefactor's head of giving me the club. From Bob Kirk it passed to his son, and from that son my benefactor bought it some thirty years ago.

There is at the moment only one tiniest drop of sorrow in my cup of happiness. I am writing from Ireland where I landed three days ago, and where I am to stay for more than another fortnight. So I shall have a weary period of waiting before I can unwrap and gaze upon my treasure. Meanwhile there is nothing to do but imagine the lovely upward curl of the shaft, and the rich oily blackness of the long thin head (or will it, by chance, be yellow?), and the fine comfortable padding of the grip that has been held by illustrious hands. The hours will pass leaden-footed till I can stroke and cherish it.

A certain anxious responsibility goes with this new possession. The putter is not to be a mere museum piece. Its owner had thought of presenting it to a club, but he says he didn't like to fancy it suspended on a club house wall, when it was still full of golfing life. Therefore, he makes it not a positive condition, but an earnest request, that its new owner shall putt with it. Needless to say, I shall comply with the request, but shall I be worthy? That is the thought that keeps me awake at night, for I cannot deny that never in my life have I used a putter rightly so called. I do putt with an aluminum club, moulded in pious imitation of the real thing, but that is the most I can say for myself. Moreover, it is impossible to conceal the fact that I am far, very far from possessing the grand manner of putting, which ought to accompany this venerable relic. Those who use putters always stand up to nearly their full height, and wield the club with a certain airy grace, whereas I am conscious of a groveling nose and bent knees and a lamentable lack of what the ancient Greeks called "arete." *Noblesse oblige* and I must clearly try to stand up and acquire a manner worthy of my putter. But an old dog cannot easily learn new tricks, and I am afraid I shall find myself stooping and groveling still. At the approach putt, I make a decent pretense of being a Scottish gentleman of the olden time, but the short ones will expose me.

A Friend of Mine
Has an Elbow

A little while ago several golfers were in danger of losing their amateur status by trying to teach golf for a monetary reward. A friend of mine, an admirable player, has an elbow. He has submitted it to the most rigorous discipline, but every now and again, and that always through sheer "cussedness" on important occasions, it insists on flying into the air at the top of his swing. After a tragic morning round he offered a handsome fee—quite a large number of pounds—to any one who could cure him, and there were many eager to earn it.

The links were dotted with physicians. Some stood close to the patient and shut one eye in a knowing manner; others stood afar off, thinking thus to gain a more comprehensive view and watched that elbow, trying to discover at what precise moment sinfulness entered into it. There were practical-minded persons, who told him to dig himself violently in the ribs at the beginning of the swing. More subtle thinkers professed to see that the poor elbow had no criminal instincts, but was forced into evil courses by that arch-crook, the body.

My own amateur conscience is clear, for having an elbow myself, I said that there was nothing for it but churchyard mould, and made no attempt to gain the reward. The end of the story cannot be told here. The patient, buoyed up by various prescriptions, went out to play nine holes. At the end of the nine his wife wanted him to come home, but he said, briefly, that he would find his own way back, and was last seen heading for the tenth green after a magnificent tee shot.

There is a temptation here to embark on a treatise about elbows. I know a picture in an old Scottish text-book, much older than that in the *Badminton*, showing a billycock-hatted gentleman at the top of his swing, with his right elbow waving high above his billycock. How much additional suffering it

210

must have caused in a suffering world! The Americans have invented a cure in the shape of a strap and buckle, which keep the elbows together. I could not afford enough dollars, but I did once truss my elbows together by means of an old tie, and thus manacled performed prodigies of skill in a lonely meadow. My friend might do worse than try this plan.

But, after all, to be captain of one's elbow is a small thing; it is a great thing to be captain of one's soul and, whatever the end of his story, he is an example of the indomitable spirit of golfers. "You can trick them and mock them with all the implements of fate—lead them on only to betray them, obsess them with hopeless dreams, punish them with senseless accidents, and harass them with wretched fears. You can buffet them, bait them, enrage them—load upon them all evils and follies in this vale of obstruction and tears. But, even at that, there is yet one thing that you cannot do. You can never make them, under any provocation, say die."

The author of *The Midnight Bell* did not write those inspiring words primarily of golfers, but of the whole race of men. I am not even sure whether he plays golf, but if he does not he has been granted, without his knowing it, the power of looking deep into their souls, for nothing truer was ever written about them. "Mock them with all the implements of fate"! Yes, indeed, think of all that steel shafts were going to do for us and yet our handicaps are still on the rise.

"Hopeless dreams and senseless accidents"! Was I not going to win that medal, if at the very first hole my ball had not kicked horribly, inexplicably, contrary to the laws of God and man, into the bunker? "Wretched fears"! Am I not so much afraid of going off at halfcock upon the green that I cannot force myself to take my putter back, but stand there transfixed and impotent? And yet, have I not just returned from practising in a muddy hayfield, where I lost several balls and grew unpleasantly warm, and do I not believe that I have found out a brand-new something? Last week I was, as a golfer, extinct; now for the hundredth time I have come to life again.

These remarks are in the first person, but they need not

have been, for they are true of all the bravest, stupidest race in the world, the unconvincible, inextinguishable race of golfers.

Only a few weeks ago I was playing in a tournament together with a very good golfer who thinks he is getting too old. He was tired out, for he had overplayed and overworked himself for other people's benefit. He almost wanted to be beaten, and when he was beaten he said that all he longed for was to put away his clubs and turn to his guns.

That was on the Tuesday night. On Wednesday his sentiments remained apparently the same, and this perfervid being actually rested. On Thursday there was a change; after a long day's watching, he sneaked out on to the lawn with a driver and some soft balls; he teed them carefully on a marked line, so as to see whether he was hitting "from the inside out," and he slogged them to the end of the lawn tennis court and back over the path and into the flower beds.

On the Friday he was busy practising with hard balls and felt once more as if he could stand up and follow though like an American. For the Saturday he had engaged to play in a four-ball match over thirty-six holes. He said he thought he could beat those two and it would be rather fun to try. I hope he succeeded, but it does not matter. He will give up the game and return to it again and again and no one will ever make him say die.

1932

To Underclub or Overclub

Which is the worse—to overclub or underclub? Superficially the question seems a foolish one, for there is no doubt which of the two faults is usually spoken of as the more criminal. Someone describing a match will say that the player underclubbed himself "scandalously" or "ridiculously" or "idiotically." The man who took too big a club is spoken of with compassion, as if he had had bad luck or a villainous caddie who misdirected him.

Perhaps the reason is that the player who underclubs himself is always suspected of vanity. We accuse him of taking too small a club in order to show how far he can hit with it; the man who takes a brassie (2 wood), when an iron would have got him there, we regard as a pleasant modest creature whose only fault is that he does not know his own strength. Generally speaking, no doubt we are right in condemning the underclubber. Habitually to take the smaller club must lead to being short, and shortness is the commonest, the most all-pervading of golfing sins.

Therefore, we ought to train ourselves into a habit of taking the bigger club. But my goodness! It does need training; it is always a difficult thing to do and sometimes it is almost impossibly difficult. If we are in some doubt as to whether we can quite get up with a particular club, we are likely to hit too hard and may make a bad shot; but if we think we shall go too far, we do not hit out at the ball, and then we are absolutely certain to make a dreadfully bad shot. I suppose that most golfers would agree that, when we are nervous, the difficulty is to hit freely, and we cannot possibly hit freely if we are obsessed with the notion that we are going too far. We wince fatally at the moment of striking. A consciously spared shot by a nervous player is more likely to reach an unreachable bunker than any other shot in the world.

This subject was put into my head by rereading the other day an article by Mr. R. E. Howard. He was writing of Mr. Bob Gardner's being beaten in our Amateur championship at Deal in 1922, largely owing to a fatally chipped mashie shot at the thirteenth hole. Mr. Gardner said he had been in two minds as to the club and then "turning to Mr. Francis Ouimet he said 'I thought of a piece of advice I once heard you give: when in doubt underclub yourself and hit with all you are worth.' And I hit so hard that my head went up and forward just too soon."

I am inclined to think that this catastrophe was the exception to Mr. Ouimet's rule. At any rate there is a good deal to be said for that rule. With the shorter club, you may very possibly top and you may hook, but you will lash out. With the longer club, if you think it is too long, you may top or hook or slice (perhaps the likeliest of all) and it is a hundred to one you won't follow through.

I know this doctrine is contrary to that which the great men preach in their books, and they are in a sense quite right. Underclubbing is a dangerous doctrine for golfing babes and sucklings. I do believe, however, that the great men sometimes deliberately disobey their own written word when it comes to the crucial point. I remember years ago Mr. Laidlay, one of the really great amateurs of a past epoch, telling me that, if at a crisis he doubted between a brassie and a cleek (2 iron), he always took the cleek even though he thought he could not get quite up, just because having to hit out with it made him feel confident. Confident! That no doubt is the point. Anything that will make us feel even moderately confident at a crisis is worth doing, however unorthodox. Yet apparently it is not the right thing to say. Mr. Laidlay never wrote a book, but if he had, I suppose he would not have said it.

There are, I imagine, even among the greatest players, those who are constitutionally underclubbers and those who are the reverse. I remember I used to regard Hagen as an underclubber. In the first championship he won at Sandwich, he astonished everybody by taking iron clubs from what seemed an almost absurd range. Sometimes he did not hit very good iron shots, but at any rate he won the championship. He won another at Sandwich a few years later and then a subtle change seemed to have come over him; he apparently was not nearly so fond of hitting his soul out and much fonder of a brassie through the green. Edward Ray I should regard as something of a champion underclubber in that he loves a lofted iron club whenever he has any pretext for using it, and the more lofted the better. The shots he used to play with his niblick (8 iron) were staggering in their impertinence. Such a heave as he used to give! Such a divot as he used to cut out! Such a height as the ball used to go! But it finished on the green.

On the other hand I should be inclined to call Harry Vardon an overclubber, but then his swing is so wonderfully smooth and rhythmic that it is—or was—almost impossible to detect him making an extra effort. Moreover, he was so astonishingly good through the green with wood, and could pick up the ball with such utter ease with that upright swing of his, that he never had the least temptation to force an iron club beyond its limits. And yet he was very long with irons at his zenith and had a driving mashie (1 iron) that he could hit as far as anybody else's brassie. Another whom I should with due humility rank among the overclubbers would be our present British Open champion, Tommy Armour. Perhaps it is his old Scottish training in the days when the half shot was considered the hall mark of the fine golfer, and there were not so many nicely graded varieties of irons. At any rate, I should judge Armour to prefer to play a shot well within himself with the longer club rather than go all out with the shorter one.

And now to which class does the immortal Bobby belong? I really do not know and I can only assume that he is the perfect golfer that belongs to neither. One thing is certain, namely, that he is, like Harry Vardon, an abnormally good judge of distance, and, I suppose, if a man can judge distance well enough, he is never in doubt between two clubs. If he is in doubt, he never seems to be and there never was a golfer who so entirely dispensed with a caddie's advice. What a blissful state!

Improving

Many years ago I used to play with a left-handed iron in order to handicap myself against an infantile sister and two small cousins. There was a certain hole which began by the bicycle shed, proceeded over and more often through a laurel-covered bank, and ended across a railing in a field between two beech trees. One great day I surmounted all these separate obstacles in one consummate stroke and finished past the beech trees. The feeling of that shot, which must have covered full ninety yards, still tingles in my memory after thirty-something years.

I even believe I can remember why I thought I had struck that ball better than any ball had ever been struck before. Because I was improving, and there is no joy comparable to that of improving. That is beyond question. When once the player has ceased to improve, then I imagine that it does not greatly matter how good or how bad he is.

There is another much humbler pleasure which yet has its points—namely, that of not having fallen off quite so much as you or your friends think you have. A recent experience has brought me a little of it, and I must say that those pattings on the back for not playing quite so badly as was expected can penetrate to the heart.

The Fête at
Puddlecombe

The postman has just brought me a document which is
not, I trust, as pathetic as it appears. In any case, some
little alteration of names and places is advisable in quoting it,
since, as Dr. Watson once remarked, "It will be obvious that
any details which would help the reader to exactly identify
the criminal would be injudicious and offensive."

This document is headed "Notice to Golfers" and announces
a fête for the church funds of, let us say, Puddlecombe. The
date, on Watsonian principles, I suppress. "There will be on
sale," it proceeds, "at attractive prices, a large number of golf
clubs by celebrated makers, part of the well known collection
of Blank, Esquire." Next come the names of the famous artists
who have fashioned the drivers, the brassies, the irons, and
the putters. These are all set out in bold black type, and then
follows, rather less conspicuously, these words: "All the above
clubs, fitted with finest selected hickory shafts. Many of them
new or little used." After the word "clubs" there is written in
ink "sixty-three in all" with two exclamation marks, and the
handwriting, shaky with emotion, is undoubtedly that of Blank,
Esquire, himself.

What can have caused the dispersal of this unique collection? Is it the hardness of the times which drives even the
richest to such heartbreaking economies as carrying their own
clubs or selling an old master? I do hope not, for I lunched
admirably with Blank, Esquire, only the other day, and it would
be dreadful to think that I had in effect been drinking his
"Iron Clubs, rustless and otherwise, by Forgan, Auchterlonie,
&c." Cleopatra and her pearl would be nothing to that. No, it
cannot be, since in that case he would surely be keeping the
profits for himself and not handing them over to the fête.

Is it, then, a sign of the remorseless advance of steel? You observed no doubt those pregnant words "all fitted with finest selected hickory shafts." Has Blank, Esquire, cast off all his faithful old friends at the caprice of this steel-hearted mistress? I know he was coquetting with steel when last I played with him. There was a clanking sound as his caddie toiled after him with a full armoury; but this is worse than anything I could have imagined.

There is a third and much less dismal possibility. It is simply this, that Blank, Esquire, in the course of a spring-cleaning at his house discovered a cache of sixty-three clubs, the possession of which he had totally forgotten, and said in an expansive moment that Puddlecombe Church might as well have them. This is on the whole the likeliest solution. It may not appear so to ordinary people, who acquire clubs on an ordinary scale, but this man has been a Maecenas of the clubmakers. He buys clubs by the dozen and hides them by fifties in a cave. There are racks of them in the passage and bags of them among the coats and hats.

As good an approaching cleek (2 iron) as I ever had—I would not insult it by calling it a jigger—I got from his pantry, not "at an attractive price," but free, handed to me with the gesture of an Oriental potentate who gives his guests any of his possessions that they admire. Mr. Boffin loved to read about the hoards of misers, how banknotes were found snug in the back of a drawer or tied up in an old jacket or in the chimney—"in nineteen different holes all well filled with soot." If Blank, Esquire's house were ransacked, goodness only knows where clubs would not be found.

He has the soul of an artist and loves a beautiful club for its own sake. He is also, as are most of us, always on the verge of discovering the great secret. When a new driver seems to have brought him for the moment nearer to his goal, he is gripped at the heart by a chill fear lest something should happen to that driver and instantly orders five more like it. Then he finds that there is a subtle lack of harmony between that driver on the one side and his brassie (2 wood) and the graduated spoons (3 wood) on the other, so the brassie and the spoons retire to the pantry to make room for a new and usurping clan.

A little later a fresh spoon seems to have possessed a certain "Je ne sais quoi" suggestion of higher things, and so, beginning at the opposite end of the scale, a similar process of discarding and refilling takes place. If the same sort of thing happens only two or three times a year in the case of a "harmonized" or "co-ordinated" set of irons, it will be understood how quickly and almost imperceptibly a house can silt up with clubs.

I have not been entirely honest about this sale. I have kept to myself one item calculated to make a collector's mouth water. I did so in the hopes of being able to attend the fête myself, but my conscience reproaches me, and, besides, I should never be able to afford it. Therefore I will reveal the fact that among the sixty-three are some "St. Andrews Wooden Putters." Moreover, these were not putters ignorantly bought off the peg; they were lovingly and leisurely fashioned to order, as the notice states, "by Jamie Anderson."

If the golfers of that most charming course at Puddlecombe are half the men I take them for they will make a rush for these treasures, and the funds of the fête will go up by great bounds. In that case it would be no more than right that there should be a little stained-glass window in Puddlecombe Church depicting Blank, Esquire, after the manner of St. Andrew, with his cross of two wooden putters. In point of fact, he uses an aluminum one today, but nobody need know that.

Our Own Paradise

I suppose every golfer in the wide world has some one golf-ing holiday spot which he loves best. He may not think it the best there is, of course, though always ready to defend it when traduced, but the going there is to him a home-coming and it gives him, not so much in the actual deed as in the anticipation, that thrill of ecstasy which grows ever rarer with the years. I have one such spot. I go there about the beginning of every year. I am counting the days now as I sit down to write and my feelings must—they really must—find an outlet in ink. This is selfish, I know, but let the reader translate my words to himself as he goes along and will not perhaps find them so tiresome. My packing, my journey, my arrival, dull in themselves, will become transmuted in his mind till they be-come his own and so of a brighter metal. He can change them one by one into his own terms so that at the end he can fancy himself arrived at his own paradise.

So then let us begin with the packing of clubs which is on such occasions a labor of love. Of course we must take more clubs than we need; the reserve must be carefully searched and it is ten to one that we find an old friend that seems by a process of resting to have become an enchanter's wand. In any case it has played on our course so often before that it would be churlish not take it there again. There was that one hole it used to play so perfectly in a cross wind—and so that good and faithful servant goes into the bag, together with two or three additional putters, although of course we should not go off our putting—Perish the thought!

I say bag, but there are some people who have a case, a vast, black case, in the nature of a sarcophagus, in which their clubs travel. It is extremely convenient, but then it has to travel apart from its owner with the guard of the train and with soul-less things like portmanteaus. I like my bag best because it is in the rack over my head and I look up at it reassuringly now and then and hug to myself the knowledge that it is really there and I am really on my way.

That brings us to the journey and so comes the weighty questions whether it is better to make it alone or in the company of other travellers to paradise. Company is a good and cheerful thing but for positive *gloating* it is almost necessary to be alone. "One of the pleasantest things in the world," says Hazlitt in a famous essay, "is going on a journey, but I like to go by myself." I am of Hazlitt's mind, or at any rate I like to start by myself.

In the earlier part of the journey I know the places to an inch; several golf courses will whirl by me and I want to look at them out of the train window—not to admire them—oh dear, no!—to despise them and to pity those who play on them, since I am bound for one so much more lovable. Poor devils! They are playing on inland mud and near smoky towns and my course is on sand within the sound of the waves. I could not say these things to the best companion in the world nor could he say them to me; it would be at once flat and childish to try. No, no. "Instead of an awkward silence (here is Hazlitt again) broken by attempts at wit or dull commonplaces, mine is that undisturbed silence of the heart which alone is perfect eloquence."

Let me make a compromise, a concession to sociability. About half way or rather further to paradise there is a junction where some of my friends, coming from other parts of the country, may join the trains. That is well, let them come! By that time, after several hours of solitary gloating, I shall be ready for them. One of the most agreeable parts of these festivals is their unchanging character and I know what we shall talk about: who are the other golfers that will be there, whether the course will be dry, whether all the new projected bunkers have been made, and then, after an interval, whether we have reached a particular little station in the hills.

It is now evening and we peer out eagerly through the window into the dark for this is of great importance. After our engine has panted up that hill it tears and rushes down into the valley with only the sea now in front of it, so that we seem in advance to sniff the salt breeze of golf.

So much for the journey, and now for the arrival. Our very last stage is along the waters of a wide estuary, and when we stop it is on the very verge of the links. We can, if we are lucky, see the sandhills looming dark and vague, and there may be a light in the clubhouse window. We leave our clubs at the station, we commit our baggage to the same old carrier with the same old horse and then set out vigorously on foot— no carriers for us!—to stump up a steep hill. The same late tea has been kept for us with the same apple jelly. We are there at last.

Almost the best is over by then for nothing can be quite as beautiful as we expect it to be. Nevertheless it is quite beautiful enough to race down that steep hill next morning. We used to do it on our feet and now I am afraid we do it in a motor car; some changes there must always be, but we get to the links and have our feet once more on that softest of seaside turf. And at the third comes that short hole over the mighty sandhill and the small caddie perched on his watch tower shouts "On the green" or sometimes he shouts "In the soup" and even that unnecessarily offensive statement does not make us very angry. We cannot get angry when we are playing golf in our own particular paradise at the start of a new year.

Winter Rules

Imitation is the sincerest form of flattery. We have for some time been flattering you Americans by our enormous sets of numbered steel shafted irons, by our pathetic attempts to swing from inside out, by our occasionally calling a bunker a trap, and now some of us have taken to winter rules. What is more, this seems to me an extremely sensible proceeding.

The same great notions seem to spring simultaneously into great minds. Some three weeks or so ago I wrote an article for an English journal suggesting winter rules for our muddier courses. I wrote it some time ahead because I was going on a holiday, and before it appeared I found it had been anticipated. Captain C. C. C. Tippet, who used to be secretary at Meadowbrook and knows much more about the subject than I do, had written an article in our *Golf Illustrated* to the same effect.

And then just about the same time, I heard that the Royal Mid-Surrey, one of the foremost clubs near London, had adopted a rule, during the winter of their discontent, that the ball should be placed through the green. This club's course in the old Deder Park at Richmond is beautifully kept but no greenskeeping, however skillful, can wholly overcome Nature, and some parts of the course do get swampy and muddy during the winter. There are in this country many clubs whose courses are far more in need of such a rule; some have already followed the good example and I have small doubt that others will do so.

It may be argued by sterner and more orthodox persons that it is "not golf" to place or tee the ball through the green, but the answer surely is that neither is it golf to play on a course where the ball lies amid worm casts and mud. As a great many people have to get their winter pleasure by playing on muddy courses, and as the game is played for pleasure, why not make the best of a bad job and get all the fun possible? There may be people whose idea of fun is to hack out of worm casts, but they are cast in heroic mould and are not, like too many golf courses, of common clay.

When a greens committee decrees winter rules it is, I assume, thinking first of the course, and no doubt the course will be very much better for lack of hacking. Captain Tippet, in his article, took the player's point of view; not that of enjoyment but the more solemn one of his education. He praised the American virtues of smooth and easy swinging *through* the ball, with no jerking or digging, and attributed that not wholly but in part to the fact of winter rules. The Englishman, he said in effect, learns to go delving for his ball at the bottom of a muddy cup and cannot get out of this vicious trick when the summer gives him good lies again. The American having in his golfing infancy been thoroughly well drilled in smoothness is never tempted by wintry conditions to abandon his good habits. This seems to me sound sense, though I fear we cannot attribute our inferiority solely to our winter golf. It is the part of anyone calling himself a golfer to learn to play out of bad lies in the proper sense of the word—a hard, bare, sandy cup or a steep hanger; but your muddy lie does not come into this category; there is no possibility of bewitching the ball out of it by timing and skill; it is merely a case for the common thud. Moreover, though it is the golfer's duty to keep his eye on the ball, he should not be punished for doing his duty by receiving on that faithful eye a piece of black and oozy mud. Neither, I am convinced, is it in any way a good or useful discipline to learn to half top his shots with the mashie (5 iron), since to touch the turf, rotten with wet, is almost necessarily fatal.

As I write these words I am conscious of advising the golfer to some extent at least to pamper himself. It would once have been considered highly immoral advice, for we used to insist in everything on the supreme value of a hard school. For instance, it was always said that only the man who had learned this game amidst tempestuous seaside gales could ever attain to quite the highest class. For a long time the records of our Open Championship seemed to prove this true, but there came our invaders from your side, bred wholly inland, who proved that they could soon grow accustomed to our sea winds and that, when they did, their truly grooved and founded swings would pull them through. A seaside education is still of value, but clearly it is not so absolutely essential and in one respect is probably detrimental.

To have to putt in youth on very keen windswept greens is too often to acquire a cramped and frightened method instead of a free, bold striking of the ball. It was Johnny Farrell, I think, most beautifully free of putters, who first made this excuse for us, and there was wisdom in his words.

When I was young I had pointed out to me the splendor of the professional who took the tiniest pinch of sand to tee his ball. To take a high tee was a sign of weakness. How could I ever learn to play my brassie (2 wood), if I pandered to my weakness by thus cocking the ball up in the air on a sand tower? Yet today I observe great men teeing the ball, figuratively speaking, mountains high, and they appear to get along very well through the green. It is all rather puzzling, but I suppose the conclusion of the whole matter is that nothing matters compared with getting ground into one's system in youth a really true and really free swing. Anything which impedes that end is bad and anything which helps towards its ultimate achievement must be reckoned as good.

1933

New Year's Eve Cheer

There is an old friend of mine with whom I have often passed New Year's Day at his pleasant house on the hill overlooking a seaside links. We drink his fine old crusted vintages, tell fine old crusted stories, play a little mild golf by day and a little, if possible, milder bridge at night. He has just written to me asking me to come again and tells me that, when I arrive, I shall find him with a beard.

That seems to me typical of the new year spirit in golfers; they have got to do something new and exciting. If the beginning of the year came in summer, they would be busy prophesying what fresh heroes would wear the championship crowns. As it comes at a dead season of golf, they are entirely occupied with their own games and the wonderful changes they are going to make in them. Here is a gentleman who up to the age of 76 or so has had a smoothly shaven chin. Now he has grown tired of it and wants a novelty; so it is a bearded chin that he will for the future, in obedience to Mr. Alex Morrison's advice, point at a spot just back of the ball.

How admirable is this youthful and adventurous spirit and yet it is one common amongst golfers. We may have come to a stage where we do not like birthdays or New Year's Day; we may pretend we are slipping slowly down the hill, and we may be quite sure that our contemporaries are doing so, but nothing can make us say die. We may not think that in the coming year we are going to be better than ever we were, but we are sure that we are going to be better than last year. That pleasantly fatuous belief never really leaves us, but it flames up more brightly than usual on the first of January, because that day is like the ninth hole in a round.

How often when we start playing very badly we say that we shall do better after the turn, and how often our words come true. We want just that definite turning point to set us on the right road and the New Year supplies us with it. On any ordinary summer day of the year if we go to bed slicers we do not expect to wake up driving with a slight, beautiful and controlled shaded draw; but as we take our bedroom candlestick with yawn on the night of December thirty-first, there seems nothing in the least improbable about such a miracle.

How grateful we golfers ought to be that our game will last us almost as long as we last ourselves, and that hope can still spring eternally in our ridiculous breasts. There comes a time of life when the sprinter realized that, if he has not run one hundred yards in ten seconds, he never will; he is done once and for all. Similarly the golfer must sometimes know, though he does not admit it, that it is extraordinarily unlikely that he will ever drive any farther than he does now. But our game holds, forever, scope for improvement in one direction: we can never chip and putt so well but that we may not learn to do it better.

No other game contains so definite, so incontrovertible a reason for cheering up and cheering up at our time in life is an incalculable blessing.

1934

Dining with the Blackheath Golf Club

The other day I had, not for the first time, the honour and pleasure of dining with the Blackheath Golf Club, the oldest golf club in the world, and it is so agreeable a function, so full of ancient and traditional observance, that some little account of it may be interesting. All the oldest and most respectable clubs seem to have had at some time disastrous fires to destroy their records—so it is no more than a legend to be respectfully believed that the club was founded in 1608 with the sanction of King James I, who played on the heath with his Scottish courtiers.

The earliest record actually existing is the silver club which was given to the society in 1776. At any rate, the seniority amongst the golfing clubs is generally conceded to the men of Blackheath, who are justifiably proud of it and are careful to maintain their dignity.

There are certain "wee" dinners (all or nearly all the original members were Scotsmen) held in the club house, but this great annual dinner is held in a London hotel. The Captain and all the past Captains wear their red tail-coats. This is a gorgeous garment with a blue velvet collar and certain agreeable blue and silver ornaments on the lapels. Also there is a single epaulet of silver. One man there is greater than any Captain, the Field Marshal. He is, as a rule, the senior among the past Captains; he holds his office not for a year but for life, and he alone of all men wears two epaulets. A good many of the members wear ordinary red golfing jackets as dinner jackets.

Before the Captain on the table lie the original silver club and its two successors of ebony and silver, to which each Captain suspends his silver ball. The older balls are, of course, smooth as were the feather balls, and some of the Captains had graven on them their crests or coats of arms. There are also on the table the various medals and prizes of the club, such as the Bombay medal, the Calcutta Cup (presents from old Scottish golfers in India) and the silver claret jug won by the famous George Glennie and Lieutenant J. C. Steward in open competition at St. Andrews in 1857, "thereby," as proudly recorded in the minutes, "constituting this club the Champion Golf Club of the world."

At the beginning of dinner the Captain reads aloud the telegram of dutiful and loyal greeting sent annually on this day to the King and the gracious answer received. After a course or two comes the Haggis, duly piped round the room by a fine figure of a piper. With the Haggis comes a loving cup of whiskey drunk out of a silver quaich. As each man drinks, his neighbours on each side stand up: he bows to each of them in turn and, when he has drunk, turns the quaich upside down to show that he has well and manfully done his duty.

After the loyal toasts comes the installment of the new Captain, and this is the great moment. The toastmaster announces that according to ancient custom the past Captains will now "proceed" round the room. The reigning Captain keeps his seat. All the others headed by the Field Marshal stand up and fall in, the new Captain coming at the end of the procession. The Field Marshal and the two senior past Captains each carry one of the silver clubs, which they wave in the air, something after the manner of a drum major. The pipes once more lead the way, and the red-coated Captains keep step on the whole pretty tolerably, being encouraged thereto by the measured clapping of the assembled company which is done in the manner called, I think, "Kentish Fire."

The procession having made the circuit halts by the Captain's chair. The reigning Captain vacates that chair, invests his successor with his medal and shakes him by the hand. Then appears the secretary to administer to the new Captain the oath of office. He addresses him in such words as these (I quote from memory) "John Smith, you have this day been appointed Captain of this ancient golf club. Will you maintain its traditions and dignities and the welfare of the game of golf?"

Then, he adds in a peremptory tone, "Kiss the club." The new Captain bows and kisses the silver club and has now entered upon his high office. His health is proposed by his predecessor, he responds and there follows the ancient toast of "Golf and Golfing Societies."

I have set down briefly what occurs but I can't hope to convey the atmosphere—the feeling that the club is a trustee of past glories and past good fellowship and is resolute to keep the trust. The club no longer plays upon the storied heath, which became altogether too full of roads and passengers and small boys playing football; its sacred soil, always somewhat hard and flinty, is cut and trampled into bareness.

So the club now plays on its private course at Eltham, which is, in point of prosaic fact, an ordinary course of the park type, though distinguished by a fine old mansion as a clubhouse. If the men of Blackheath, when they left the heath after playing there more than three hundred years, had shown any tendency to forget their tradition, they might have lapsed into an ordinary London club—been lost among the multitude of their neighbors; but they have done nothing of the sort; they have jealously guarded every observance and as long as they do that their place and dignity are secure.

Exactly a hundred years before the dinner I have described there was another dinner and the record of it in the club annals is so true today that I can't do better than end with it. "Eighteenth October 1834. The vocal strength of the Club was eminently conspicuous this evening, and the meeting altogether found so delightful, that it will not easily be surpassed in our Golfing Annals."

Out of Bounds

"**W**ell, you knew it was there. You ought to have gone somewhere else." That is the answer that we have often made, not perhaps aloud but in the recesses of our own minds, to an adversary who has bemoaned a ball which has just trickled into an unkind bunker or just hopped out of bounds. No doubt also our enemy has often made it to us when it has been our turn to call gods and men to witness the gross unfairness of the world.

It played its part in a discussion during the Easter holidays, which were so much better suited to talking about golf than to playing it. There were four of us, and one, who has the power of life and death at a particular course, invited our considered judgments as to whether the fourth hole would be better, if the penalty for out of bounds were reduced from stroke and distance to the loss of distance only.

We all had the conviction that he would do what he thought best in his dictatorial mind whatever our opinions might be, but still we were flattered at being asked. So we did our best, and, as in the case of the three jovial huntsmen, the first said one thing and the second another, and "the other he said nay." One wanted to make the penalty half a stroke and all the distance, and we all shouted him down. He protested that he did not see why it was impossible, but we just said: "Away with it," and gave no reasons. Another wanted to keep the rule as it is—namely, the rule of golf, which prescribes the loss of stroke and distance; but he admitted a sneaking desire to keep the full penalty only when the hole was played from the back tee, and to be more lenient in the case of the forward tee. His *ratio decidendi*, if I have the expression aright, was that the longer the hole the better the chance of catching up, whereas at a shorter hole the full penalty almost inevitably meant the loss of the hole.

Then came my turn, and I began by trying to sit on the fence. I said that as there were so few chances of going out of bounds on this particular course I thought the full penalty should be retained; if it had been Hoylake, where there are almost endless possibilities, loss of distance was enough. I was proceeding to add an interesting story about a friend of mine who, in the course of an ill-spent life, had been out of bounds at every single hole at Hoylake except the Rushes, when I was brought ruthlessly back to the point.

The dictator said to me, as Mr. Pickwick did to Sam on the shooting expedition: "Kindly reserve your anecdotes till they are called for." What he wanted to know was whether this single hole would be better under one rule or under the other.

I was frightened nearly out of my wits and tried to think not what was my own truthful opinion, but what was the answer he would like. He is a gentleman of strongly conservative views, a hater of local rules, and I could hardly imagine that he would allow any concession to southern weaknesses. But in that case what was there in his vast and brooding mind, and why had he asked us the questions?

Finally, stammering and blushing I voted for the loss of distance only, and—I had guessed right. He admitted that he stood aghast at his own moderation, that his views had undergone a surprising change, and that he now thought that the hole would be "better sport" under the milder penalty.

I have been wondering since whether he and I—for what I am worth, which is very little—are right. It is a difficult question. At present, if the player who has the honour goes out of bounds, he will probably take six to the hole, and the other man, by a series of more or less ignominious scuffles and scrambles to the left, can comfortably get his five and win the hole; only the truly heroic on one side, or the ineffably futile on the other, can prevent such an ending; when the first ball soars away on to the railway line the hole is to all intents and purposes over.

On the other side there is that good old solid argument that the player knows the railway is there and goes near it at his peril. Is there not something more besides, a consideration not merely of hard justice, but of natural, human pleasure? At present, if I can steer my ball close to the railway, I derive from the feat a positively glowing satisfaction. And, alternatively, if I pull away safely to the left I can still pat myself on the back for having used my head and refused to be tempted to my destruction.

It is the imminence of the peril, the terrible severity of the punishment avoided, that give to my feelings such a delicious poignancy. "Envy me, sir," I say with Mr. Malthus in "The Suicide Club." "Envy me, I am a coward." In proportion as the peril and the punishment are decreased so will my blissful relief be decreased also, for to fear death is truly to taste the joys of living.

The hole in question—you can see it from the train on your way to Southampton—is in design and conception very like the sixteenth hole at St. Andrews. If my friend held that gorgeous hole in fee, would he, I wonder, contemplate reducing the penalty for going into the railway there to loss of distance only? He would not. His conservative instincts would be too much for him. It might possibly be inconsistent, but that would not matter. He would take the strong line, and afterwards, like Frederick the Great, would find some pedant to point out why he was right.

Right, in my humble judgment, he would be. To flout the railway and the Principal's Nose, to forget all about Deacon Slime and to fare unscathed down that narrow way, gives to life a zest so intense that surely nothing should be allowed to diminish it. No, when I think of the Corner of the Dyke, I am all for the rigour of the game, and almost hope that my friend may return to his older and fiercer opinions.

The Uniqueness of the Old Course

What is a good length hole? I imagine that if there were such things as examinations in golf, and that question was set, we can be sure of the answer that the orthodox, well-crammed student would give. He might quote the now ancient words of the *Badminton* volume in praise of St. Andrews: "The holes are so disposed that they may be reached with two, or maybe three, real good drives."

That still holds as a definition of "good length" holes in general, but is not any longer a true description of the holes at St. Andrews. I have lately returned from a few days at that noble place. The ground was hard and dry and full of running, and the only holes that could be said to require "two really good drives" were those which once—in gutty days—required three of them. It is one of the ironies of golf that this should be so. At the same time, it is one of the greatest testimonies to the course's greatness that it does not matter. Instead of proving, as it was once held to do, the merits of the good length hole, it now proves that—at St. Andrews—there is no such thing as a bad length hole.

I have often been asked by friends in America, who have never been there, what is the quality that makes the Old Course unique, and I have made but a poor hand at the answering. It is, I think, as far as it is at all definable, this indestructible nature of the length of the holes. Why is it that approaches of nondescript length are so infinitely more interesting at St. Andrews than on (with all possible respect to them) other courses? Simply because in dry weather the approaches have to be infinitely more accurate.

In its most charitable moods, the ground never helps the player and that is an immense virtue. When the ground is hard, it is not merely unhelpful, it is "aye fechtin' against ye."

The result is that the smallest inaccuracy with a short approach may leave the player twenty, yes, and thirty and forty yards from the pin, to struggle in agony for his four. One friend of mine lamented after the Medal that he had taken forty-nine putts. The number is certainly excessive, and I am quite ready to concede that he cannot have putted very well, but I don't believe he could have approached very well either.

The second shot to the tenth hole may serve as an illustration, though, of course, only those who know it can thoroughly appreciate it. Here is a hole only some three hundred yards long. Big hitters can reach the green now and then with their tee shots; the humblest can get so near that the second shot appears only to consist in a knock along the ground with "any old club." Yet here is one of the most fascinating and exacting little shots in existence. The amount of latitude allowed is not more than a foot or so either way.

It may be complained by those, who like perdition on a tremendous scale, that nothing much happens if the player does not go straight enough. True, the ball does not plunge into cavernous bunkers, but what happens is that it flies away from the hole on wings of the most impish malice and exaggerates the crookedness of the shot to an incredible degree. The hole does worse than punish a man; it makes him ridiculous.

There was an American friend of mine there this year. He was a new member of the Royal & Ancient Club and this was his first visit, but he had read and heard so much beforehand that he could tell the name of every bunker even as his ball was speeding toward it for the first time. He had only one gentle complaint, he had been there for nearly a week and with only one round left to play he had never yet been into Strath, perhaps the most famous—or infamous—bunker of them all. His unspoken prayer was answered and with the last tee shot to the eleventh hole in he went, and, what was more, his ball lay impossibly tucked up under the overhanging brink, so that he could scarcely stand or play his club. With a radiant countenance he plunged in after it and it was only with his fifth thump that he got it out. Then he felt for the first time that he had won his spurs and been given the freedom of the Old Course.

He and I came away from St. Andrews together and sat for sometime on my bed in the sleeping car talking it all over again. There were many other golfers on that train and there was not one of us, I suppose, who had not in the last day or two called Gods and men to witness that the course was grossly unfair. Neither was there one of us that two minutes later had not been analyzing yet again the surpassing greatness of it—the most damnable and infinitely the most lovable links in the world.

An Era
Passes with Kirkaldy

St. Andrews was gay and festive as ever for the Walker Cup matches, but there was something lacking, and one felt it distinctly. Andrew Kirkaldy was not there. This was the first great occasion for many a day on which poor old Andrew had not walked out—with increasing difficulty each year, but, if possible, with ever augmented dignity—to hold the flag on the home green. For such was the proud prerogative of this *doyen* of old school professionals who was one of the most colorful characters ever associated with St. Andrews. The place will not seem at all the same without him, and I may perhaps add this one small personal word. I have just had paid to me the most pleasant honor of being made Captain-elect of the Royal and Ancient Club. When, if all is well, I drive myself into office next September I shall be the first Captain for a long time that has not had Andrew to tee his ball for him.

Andrew was 74 when he died, had long been looked upon as the last of the 19th Century professionals and had already in his lifetime become a great legendary figure. Incidentally, it became part of the legend, as purveyed by English newspaper writers, that he be called "Andra." Why I know not, for I never met an educated Scotsman who called him anything but "Andrew." He had become so famous as a figure and a character that people had begun to forget that he had been a very, very fine player. As long ago as 1879, before he enlisted and fought at Tel-el-Kebir, he had been second, as a boy, in the Open Championship. He never won it but he tied for it with Willie Park ten years later, lost the tie and then destroyed his conqueror in a great private match over four greens. That and his victory over J. H. Taylor at St. Andrews in the 1890s were the matches he liked best to look back upon, and match play was his game. Not for Andrew to play the cold, impersonal game against par. His was a fierce, hostile spirit that revelled in the man-to-man, hand-to-hand encounter, that watched the enemy as the cat does a mouse, and loved to pounce at the right moment. "The door's locked now," he shouted as he holed a putt at the corner of the Dyke to make him dormie two in a big match against Andrew Scott. That was typical. He had got his enemy under his heel and saw no reason to conceal his joy. If the other man did not like it he must lump it.

There was something most daunting in Andrew's manner of playing a match and likewise in his manner of hitting the ball. He rather "sat down" to it with an air of formidable and deliberate purpose, and then back went the club like a streak of lightning, the swing was rather short and quick, but the blow itself was wonderfully firm and solid, and no man ever hit a ball more cleanly. It was like the shutting of a knife. He revelled in a wind and was a consummate master of all the running shots which St. Andrews demands and used to demand more imperatively, owing to the bareness and keenness of the course in Andrew's best days. "You were quite wrong, Kirkaldy," said an English visitor who thought he had been misdirected by his foursome partner, "a ball won't run up that bank." "By God," was the uncompromising answer, "if I had hit that ball it would have run up the bank." And so it would. Over would have come that mighty right wrist with the action known as "locking the door" and the obedient ball would have climbed the plateau without faltering and run on to lie near the pin. Andrew was better at home than anywhere else, and he was one of those who regarded a comparison of any other links with St. Andrews as blasphemy.

I have described Andrew's method of playing as "hostile" and so it was; when he was in one of his growling moods he was undoubtedly alarming, but he mellowed as he grew older and moreover, under that fierce outside, there was a great deal of kindliness and friendly human nature. It must be remembered that he began life when there was for such as him little or no education. When the golf professional was scarcely removed from the caddie, and had a hard struggle for life. So

Andrew was rough but he had also many of the qualities of the diamond; he grew old gracefully, with no jealousy of those of a generation to whom fell richer prizes, and the older he grew the fonder did everybody grow of him. He was no kind of courtier; he bowed no knee and he spoke to everyone and anyone in the same direct uncompromising manner. He never would have acknowledged it, perhaps, but I think he would have been a little proud and pleased if he had foreseen his own funeral with the silver cup draped in black and the Captain and Ex-Captain of the Royal and Ancient in procession behind it.

There are, of course, endless stories about Andrew, some true and some not. One or two worshippers at his shrine have, I believe, made a collection of them in books that will never see the light. I am not going to try to tell them because I am not well enough versed in the Fife tongue and because in the best of them the *mot juste* has nearly always to be left out. Andrew was a little too—shall we say, racy?—for print. He gained, in a sense unreservedly, the reputation of a wit. A wit, I take it, says things that he intends to be amusing or biting. Andrew said what he thought in ferocious earnest, without meaning to be amusing at all. He had a natural trenchancy of diction that made his remarks amusing despite himself. He knew, no doubt, that he was regarded as a "character," but I do not think he tried to live up to it; he just said what he thought simply and decidedly and could not help saying characteristic things. There used to be more like him at St. Andrews and there are still a few, but Andrew was the strongest, most individual, and most typical of the long ago race of professionals and "hath not left his peer."

1935

Those Red Coat Days

The May medal day at St. Andrews was as cold and cheerless as need be, indeed a little further north, at Aberdeen, snow was falling and lying. So it seemed as if sudden warmth and sunshine had come to cheer us when there walked into the clubhouse a gentleman in a bright scarlet coat. For a moment he appeared to be some ghost from the red-coated past but he was nothing of the sort, he was Lord Kinnaird, the reigning Captain of the Royal Perth Golfing Society.

His collar was of royal blue velvet and his gold buttons were adorned with the insignia of that ancient and illustrious club. He not only wore his coat in the clubhouse but he went out to play his medal round in it and the splash of scarlet on the green made people think how pleasant a sight an old medal day must have been when it was every gentleman's duty to appear in his club uniform.

It is strange that the red coat has so utterly disappeared off the face of the earth, for it is the old and traditional uniform of the game. It is recorded in the minutes for 1780 of the St. Andrews Golf Club (it was not Royal and Ancient then) that "The Society took into their consideration that their golfing jackets are in bad condition—Have agreed that they shall have new ones viz Red with yellow buttons. The undermentioned gentlemen have likewise agreed to have an uniform frock—viz a buff colour with a red cap, the coat to be half lapelled, the button white. Balcarres and ten others."

Very smart they must have looked, especially Lord Balcarres and his ten fellow-exquisites when they all appeared simultaneously in their new raiment. Yet they were not unique either at that time or for a long time afterward. In 1837 at Musselburgh Mr. John Wood of the Honourable Company of Edinburgh Golfers was "fined two tappit hens for appearing on the Links without a red coat."

About the same time the Scottish Patriots and exiles who played their national game on Blackheath decided that "the uniform (beside the jacket) be a buff waistcoat and black hand-kerchief" and some twenty years later, in 1856, it was recommended that every member should wear the Club uniform when playing on "Club days."

It is not necessary, though it is fascinating, to go nearly so far back. I myself—moi qui vous parle—have possessed a red coat and mightily proud of it I was when I first bought it, for it had a light blue collar and the arms of Cambridge blazing with gold and ermine on the pocket, and signified that I had been chosen to play against Oxford.

Ten years or so before that, when I first began as a small boy to play golf, in point of fact fifty years ago now, more people wore red coats than not and the eager neophyte would wonder whether he was now a sufficiently good player so to adorn himself. There used to be a sort of myth to the effect that a man who had got round in under 100 could so far presume.

Then gradually the custom began to die out for no ostensible reason. It was dying steadily in the 1890s for I remember that in my first championship in 1898 one player in a red coat looked a little singular. Once the twentieth century was in its stride, I think the red coat had been decently interred except on one or two public courses where it was worn as a danger signal to avoid being pelted by errant drives.

Why did it depart? The golfer of today will be inclined to think that it was because men gave up the habit of playing in coats of any hue and took to loose and comfortable jerseys and pull-overs. That certainly was not the reason. The eminently sensible golfing costume of today (though I still like a coat best) came to us much later, chiefly, I fancy, through American influence.

It was no objection to coats in themselves, it was merely that fashion, with its inscrutable decrees, set against red coats; the "best people" ceased to wear them and the humble fry, who a few years ago had been so eager for red coats and facings of blue and green and yellow, followed suit. Today it is still the traditional uniform for dinner of the Captains of certain clubs, but except for that it is rarely seen.

There were some admirers of Lord Kinnaird's coat at St. Andrews who talked of starting a crusade to bring red coats back, to enter into a compact, as did Lord Balcarres and the ten other gentlemen one hundred and fifty-five years ago. Unless I am much mistaken they will never do it. It is one of the things that is pleasant to talk of doing. If they buy coats they will come to wear them, as members of the Royal Blackheath Club often do, simply as short dinner jackets to be worn with a black tie.

At any rate I do not feel brave enough or enthusiastic enough to become a crusader. My old coat has gone long since, the victim of a moth or of a house-moving, no man can say whither, and, if it had not, I am afraid I could no longer get into it. It was a thing of beauty in its day, but its day is past. At least I think so, but I half hope I am wrong, for the red did look pretty against the green.

A Golf Writer's Revenge

I am writing this article a little before its time because I am going for my holiday. I don't want to work more than I can help on a holiday; I do want to gloat about it beforehand. Just once a year seems to me a not excessive allowance in the matter of gloating. Moreover, though I may seem to be selfish, am I not putting myself in sympathy with all the world because all the world has a holiday.

At this moment I am thinking about a train from Kings Cross Station, about Berwick and the silvery Tweed far below us. Thinking about the Forth Bridge and the change at Leuchars Junction and finally the last little bit of the journey in the little local train which will bring me curving into St. Andrews, right along the edge of the links. Well, my readers, if I have any, can translate that heavenly journey of mine into their own language. Their journey will have different landmarks and will take them to a different paradise, but it will be essentially the same and at the end of it they will find, just as I hope to do, their own familiar friends plying their niblicks in familiar bunkers.

There is, indeed, one aspect of a golfing holiday which does not appeal to all but does to this poor golfing writer. That is the blissful thought that he is going to play golf without having to write about it. I suppose all of us, who are not saints and angels but reasonably malignant human beings, habitually heighten the joys of a holiday by thinking about other people who have already had theirs and gone back to work. As we loaf gently down to the clubhouse after a late breakfast with the prospect of two good rounds before us, we reflect, not in a wholly Christian spirit, that they are at the moment catching their daily-bread trains to their offices. I am going to revel in this discreditable delight in its most poignant form.

THE HAPPY GOLFER

During my first two weeks at St. Andrews there will be two competitions, the Jubilee Vase and the Calcutta Cup. Not only shall I not have to report them but I shall, with my own eyes, see somebody else having to do so. When I have finished playing or watching I shall be able to take my ease and my drink while I watch the other poor fellow button-holing competitors, asking them how they fared, listening to their tales of woe, making hasty notes which he will not afterwards be able to read and ultimately retiring to a corner laboriously to write his story. Could anything be more maliciously agreeable than that? It is as if the office worker on a holiday could, by means of television, actually see his fellows toiling in black coats and hot cities. At such a moment I could almost exclaim to the rest of the world "Envy me, sirs, I am a golfing writer!"

It is of course a sad commonplace about a golfing holiday that the best part of it is the looking forward to it, the second best the packing for it, and the third best the journey, and the fourth best the holiday itself. Can any perfectly truthful man lay his hand on his heart and say that he has ever played as well on his holiday as in his dreams he thought he was going to play? Disappointment begins, as a rule, on the very first blissful day of all. We may not have been playing much beforehand, but we have practised putting on the domestic course on the lawn, pitching over the flower beds and driving in the neighboring meadow.

For each of those arts we have got a new theory and new theories are wonderfully effective on a lawn or in a field with nobody to look at us. The moment we come on to a real course there is a subtle but definite change in the atmosphere; light, wind, turf, everything is different. We imagine that we shall be perfectly at home and in fact we feel perfectly strange. We realize yet once more that domestic practise is better than none at all but not a substitute for practise in a game and on a links. The disappointment is the keener because our hopes have been so absurdly high, and we shall be fortunate if every one of those theories has not been abandoned before the first nine holes are out.

This anguish does pass off. For a day or two we are like the small child who, because he is not allowed a particular piece of cake, thinks drearily that there will never be any cake again in the world. Then just because we are getting familiar with the feel of the club we find ourselves playing rather well and then comes the really crucial moment—are we going to get stale? Judiciously to ease off just when we are as we say "coming on to it" requires sometimes a fierce effort of will, but if we do not make that effort we shall probably have sad things to suffer. It will be harder to play well later on because the dreadful part of staleness is this, that we hate the game and yet cannot bear to give it up. It becomes a deadly drug from which we cannot refrain even though we know it is destroying us. Even if we do succeed in taking a day off our mind is occupied with new and complicated theories for the next morning. The time to take it easy is when we have a system, however fallible, which is producing satisfactory results. Then our mind is at peace, we can spend a whole day vacantly throwing stones into the sea and return to the links genuinely refreshed.

I have preached a sermon of this sort to myself before many holidays and seldom conformed with my own doctrines. What will happen this time? Meanwhile I have a theory, and it is high time that I went out into the field and tried it.

"Where the Music Ought to Be"

Golfing fashions are like the fleeting clouds, so swiftly do they come and go. Pigmy shafts and immense "Dreadnoughts" of five and forty inches, pudgy little bulldog heads and those vast heads called "baps," to which old Andrew Kirkaldy perpetuated an historic if impolite similitude—we have tried them all and they have passed. In writing of our latest fashion I may be, for aught I know, late for the fair; the American continent may already be in its grip, but I must take the risk. At the moment all England, or at any rate all middle-aged England, is experimenting in trembling hope with the "limber" shaft.

This is simply a shaft of excessive springiness with the spring not merely near the head, where old Tom Morris used to say the "music" ought to be, but all-pervading. It seems to have come upon us quite quickly, for the first time I heard the name or handled one of these clubs was at Rye in January, when Roger Wethered, of all people, proceeded to drive well enough to win The President's Putter again. I was told that Braid had taken to one, Braid, the "divine fury," whose hitting was proverbial. So has Sand Herd, so has another illustrious veteran, Edward Ray, and all three, if one can believe what one is told, feel that they have renewed their youth.

Sandy alleges that once more he can get the little draw that means so much; Ray that his game has come back to him with a rush. And not only these famous people but many of the middle-aged rank and file profess to have derived all manner of benefit. Some of them are players with a naturally leisurely method such as the club would be expected to suit, but others are by nature rapid and violent hitters, not at all conspicuous for rhythmic beauty of method. To them, too, it seems, has been vouchsafed this elixir of youth.

252

BERNARD DARWIN

My own humble experience, for what it is worth, has been at once gratifying and disappointing. I admit that I have only indulged in a little practice in a meadow and the result is entirely different from what I imagined. I fancied that I should produce some desperate hooks, some ludicrous slices, but that now and again the ball would sail with supreme dominion far beyond my ordinary limits. On the contrary, the club seems to present no astonishing difficulty; it performs no prodigies of eccentricity, but, alas! neither does it produce prodigies of (relative) length. In short it behaves no better and not noticeably worse than my normal club.

On the other hand I did find, and so others have found, one pleasing consequence. Using this slippery eel of a club seems to have put my ordinary, pedestrian club upon its good behavior. It was as if the old and tried friend was made jealous by the intrusion of this newcomer. There it stood neglected against the railings at the end of the meadow, and there was its faithless master marching up and down and totally neglecting it, while he clasped in his hand this new-fangled upstart. "Very well," said the old favorite. "I'll show him," and when it was again given a chance it hit the ball with a dash and vigor which had long since seemed to have departed from it.

Muirfield in Winter

A great many American golfers have been to Scotland in summer, but I suspect very few have been there in winter. Neither, I have now come to believe, have many Englishmen. Till lately I myself have been nothing but a summer tripper and when a kind friend asked me to come and stay in February I told several English golfers rather shamefacedly that I had never been to Scotland in winter before. To my surprise most everyone answered "No more have I" and I began to be less ashamed of myself. The going was a great romance and I thought of little else for several days beforehand. Now I have come home again; I am hugging to myself the memory of three of the most delightfully friendly and sunshiny days of golf I have ever had in my life and, however tiresome I may be, I cannot help talking about them.

My friends and my family prophesied the gloomiest things for me. They said that it would probably snow, that it would certainly freeze hard, and they urged me so strongly to take all the thick clothes I had ever possessed that I began to feel like an arctic explorer. In vain did I quote my host's letter that his wife had lately picked a bunch of roses in her garden at North Berwick. This statement was received with ribald Saxon merriment. I dined at my club before catching my night train and when I rose to go with the statement that I must be off for Scotland I was overwhelmed with that kind of sympathy which takes a pleasure in its friend's misfortunes. Well, I have the laugh of them all now, for it froze and it snowed in London while I was basking in my Riviera of Muirfield.

It is always an exciting moment to wake up in Scotland, to look out of the window and to see everywhere the running waters; they were streams in England and now they are burns. It was more than ever thrilling this time and, Heaven be praised, there was never a patch of snow even on the hills, and not as much as a puff of bitter wind to ruffle the trees. By half past ten o'clock I was in the delicious solitude of Muirfield, with the sun just coming through a thin veil of mist, playing golf, and without my waistcoat. There was to be sure a little frost in the ground and our early putts behaved rather eccentrically while our driving powers were flattered.

By noon the frost had all gone and for the rest of my three days the weather was perfect. I really mean perfect because to my mind winter golf in fine weather on a seaside course is the best that life has to offer, and worth a hundred rounds on summer days. There is a freshness about the turf as about the air which summer cannot give, and the holes are of the right length. We cannot reach the greens by means of senile shuffles which send the ball much further than they deserve. The ball "maun be hit," we hit it as well as we can and if ever we succeed how great is our reward and our joy. The Open championship is at Muirfield this year and doubtless the professionals will be compassing the "two-shot" holes with a vast driver and then a flick with some much lofted club. In winter, they might occasionally have to use a wooden club for their second shots and lash out like men to get home.

I went to Scotland not only to play my games but to be a guest at dinner of that venerable and illustrious club, the Honorable Company at Edinburgh Golfers, whose home is Muirfield. The members dine periodically, make matches—nearly all of them foursomes—and if they have a mind to it bet on them in moderation. There is at once great friendliness and a pleasant air of ceremony and tradition. Several members may rise simultaneously to catch the eye of the Captain in his red coat who sits entrenched behind the Silver Club, with silver balls depending from it. "Mr. So and So," says the great man, whereupon Mr. So and So delivers himself as follows: "Mr. Captain, with your permission Mr. A and I propose to play Mr. C and Mr. D on Saturday, the ninth of February." There ensues a few minutes of babel in which bets are made and then the Captain hammers on the table with his mallet of office, silence falls, the recorder rises and says, "Sir, the match is Mr. A and Mr. B against Mr. C and Mr. D" and reads out all the wagers that have been laid. Then more people leap respectfully to their feet, another match is read out and so the match-making goes busily and cheerfully along. Let me add in modest parenthesis that a match was made for me and that with a stout partner I managed to win it.

I could enlarge forever on the beauty of those days, on Gullane Hill and the view over the misty sea and the mystery of Archerfield wood with its gnarled fir trees permanently heeling over under the wind, the wind which comes into Robert Louis Stevenson's great story, "The Pavilion on the Links." However, this is not business and since Muirfield is the scene of the championship, in which I hope we shall have some American champions playing, I may say that the course has been in several ways changed and improved since Walter Hagen won there in 1929. Incidentally, Hagen himself has caused one change, for he exploited an ingenious short cut to the eighth hole, by way of the rough, which was not rough enough, and now they have planted a hedge there to stop such antics.

A variety of unsightly and superfluous bunkers have been filled up and one or two small but dominating ones put in. The first hole, for instance, which was dull and straight, with rows of bunkers on either hand, has now the most ingenious little fellow in front of the green. The man who drives to the left has a straight run for his second. The man who drives to the right will have to play his second with an extremely skillful slice. Then the bunkering has been altered at the home hole, which is now closely beset and makes a splendid ending.

Most important of all the horrid, ugly little thirteenth, which looked as if it came out of a suburban garden, has been done away with and a really fine, dangerous, uphill, one-shot hole substituted. I admit the old one did cause dramatic disasters, but it was a scurvy little beast and I am thankful it is gone. Altogether I think Muirfield will make a fine battlefield when the day comes, but it never can be quite so good again as it was on those winter days "sent from beyond the skies."

Limitation of Armaments

The subject of limitation of armaments is in the air just now and has penetrated to the golf course. Not indeed for the first time, for various people, and in particular Mr. Chick Evans, have been preaching for some time; but I think theirs are not so palpably voices crying in the wilderness as they used to be.

It seems appropriate to receive a letter about disarmament from an eminent soldier, and I have just had one, apropos of something I wrote, from a General, but a good golfer, bred on a famous links and one of a famous brotherhood of golfers. He says that for many years before the war and a little while after it his equipment consisted of six clubs—driver, brassie, mid-iron, mashie, mashie-niblick and a putter; he adds that his brassie was rather more lofted that the "full-blooded instrument of today."

It was two years or so after the war that the disintegration of his morale began. A professional recommended him to buy a No. 4 iron because "it was so easy to play with" and he succumbed. Then the *facilis descensus* began until two years ago he fell to a complete matched and steel-shafted set with irons numbered from 2 to 8. Now he announces to me his intention of repenting and going back to his old ways and his old set of clubs. I have begged him to tell me how he fares that I may make a propagandist article out of him. Meanwhile a propagandist letter was written to the *Times* by a gentleman of eminence in a more peaceful walk of life, Mr. O. T. Falk, who used to be a good golfer and is now a very good economist. As befits an economist he is thinking of the time when "the reorganization of the social structure" (a truly formidable expression!) shall have proceeded much further and in a more drastic manner than it has up till now. Golf in its expensive and complex form will, according to his prophecy, become impossible, and he proposes to anticipate that time by a legal limitation of the number of clubs to three. "There is much to be said," he adds, "for only one."

Taking rather less long views I wish he had not proposed such a root and branch policy, which will for the moment have few adherents. One club is altogether out of the realm of practical politics. Nearly all of us would have to make our one club an iron and, beautiful and fascinating though iron play is, the loss of the sweet sensation of hitting with wood would take something from the game for which nothing could make amends. As Mr. Hutchinson once wrote, if there were no driving there would be very little golf. Even three clubs is far too jejune an allowance to satisfy all save epicures in golf. My friend the General's six clubs constitute a real practical possibility, and there is no very obvious gap in his list, except that something in the nature of a driving iron as well as his "mid-iron" might surely be permissible. Reforms must be made by easy stages and for my part, were I a reforming dictator, I would begin by allowing the golfer at the least ten clubs. It is difficult to believe that there is any shot on any golf course that cannot be played by a competent golfer with one of ten clubs.

It may be said at once that, leaving on one side the humanitarian question of the over-burdened caddie, the main and perhaps the only argument in favor of limitation is an aesthetic one; it would make of golf, as elder players think at least, a prettier game demanding a higher and more varied standard of accomplishment from the player. Incidentally it would make it a less ridiculous one, because there is surely something ridiculous in the sight of a man diving into a bag like a sarcophagus to search for one of some twenty or more clubs. The change that would come over the game cannot be better or more tersely stated than in Mr. Falk's own words. "Uniformity of the hitting method and great variety of club face are replaced by greater uniformity of club face and variety of method of hitting." That a game so played would be more fascinating I do not think anybody can doubt who remembers golf as it was played, let us say, in the Vardonian era.

Today we praise, and rightly, somebody's beautiful method of swinging the club. In older days we had the additional interest of studying and admiring the great men's particular ways of playing particular shots. There were half-shots, push-shots or what not; today there is by comparison one shot and golf is the duller for it. Opinions will naturally differ as to the value to be attached to these aesthetic arguments, but I do not think they should be lightly set aside. It is very easy in this world to think too much of the purely "practical" side of a question.

There is an objection to the limitation of clubs which always worries me personally: it would be an interference with the liberty of the golfing subject. In its essence golf has always been a free game. The golfer was originally given a ball and permitted to get it into the hole with any kind of implement that seemed best to him. That freedom has had to be curtailed in some directions owing to the misplaced ingenuity of people who desired to "merchandise" golf, but still in the larger sense freedom remains a feature of golf and in some ways it would be a pity if it were further diminished.

My own impression, for what it is worth, is that we shall all talk a good deal about this reform and never quite do anything. Moreover, the longer reform is put off the less likely in some ways it is to come, because those who knew the beauties of the old game will not be here forever to preach about them, and a generation that has always known a multiplicity of clubs will see no particular reason for a change. So perhaps the change will only come naturally and inevitably through the "reorganization of the social structure" with which Mr. Falk threatens us. By the time we are reduced to his one club I fancy my only club, if any, will be a putter and I am content that it should be so.

1936

A Town on the Sand

This was Darwin's final article (January 1936) for The American Golfer *magazine. The Great Depression had taken its toll on both golf and the magazine. The January 1936 issue was its last.* The American Golfer *was absorbed into the old* Sports Illustrated *in February 1936.*

The other day I made a brief raid into Devonshire to revisit one of the most magnificent pieces of golfing country in the world, at Saunton which is near Westward Ho! The secretary there told me a pleasant little story. When Saunton was first opened the great James Braid came down to play in the first competition. He did rather a poor score taking an eight at one hole and my friend said to him a little apprehensively, "What do you think of the course?" "It's no' a course," Braid answered. The poor secretary, now feeling thoroughly miserable, began to ask humbly what was the matter with it when he observed a benignant smile upon the great man's face. "You misunderstand me," he said. "It ought never to be called a course. It's a links and one of the very few real links left."

No course (I must use the word) could have a better or truer compliment. Saunton does still possess the old natural seaside quality which owing to the inevitable over-civilization and over-cultivation of golf is very rarely found. The moment one sets eyes on it one feels that all that is necessary is to mark a few whitewash lines for teeing grounds, dig some holes almost anywhere among the hills and valleys and go out to play. The sight of it took me back to far off days of schoolboy golf. I used as a boy to get down to Felixstowe just as the dusk was coming on and would instantly rush out without as much as changing my shoes to have a few thrilling shots. I go to Saunton rather late on a dark winter afternoon with a wind blowing fiercely in from the sea and a black sky full of rain. Save that I was some five and forty years older I felt just as I used to do at Felixstowe. I must have some shots before the light faded and out I went solitary and happy. I remember having just the same feeling when, with Mr. C. B. Macdonald, I first came to the National as the sun was setting. There are very, very few courses that can produce it, but to experience it is one of the greatest ecstasies that golf has to offer.

When I first went to Saunton ten years ago it had one course. Now it has two and for that matter it might have half a dozen. Towering mountains and deep crevasses of sand, smiling valleys and plains of turf (which are covered in the spring with the loveliest flowers) stretch away into the distance as if there were no end to them. The place somehow suggests that deep below the towering and tumultuous hills there must lie buried a vanished civilization, nor is the suggestion altogether ill founded. A pleasant old Devon antiquary, Tristram Risdon, who lived in the seventeenth century wrote of it: "Saunton, not inaptly so termed the Town of the Sand, that hath overblown many hundreds of acres of land. And near this hamlet the country people had so undermined a hill of sand by digging it to carry it into their grounds, that a great quantity thereof fell down, discovering the top of a tree, which, by further search, was found to be thirty feet in length, so that it plainly appeareth this circuit of marsh land was in elder ages stored with wood and tall timber." He goes on to talk of a little solitary church of his day, St. Anne's Chapel, very near the sea which "doubts not drowning, so much as the swallowing up of the sand, driven by drifts of the north-west winds, stirring storms and playing the tyrant in this tract." That wind has done its work long since, the little chapel is engulfed and there is nothing there but the greedy sand. Nothing, that is to say, but one old blackened wreck of a sycamore tree on the crest of a sand hill which acts as our guide flag at one hole. Perhaps it is the solitary survivor of all that "tall timber" which according to our antiquary lies buried below.

I could not resist those quotations, they seem to me extraordinarily romantic and Saunton is a most romantic place in which to play golf. It possesses everything on a fine big scale—gorgeous hills and wastes of sand to drive over, tall clumps of spiky rushes of the Westward Ho! brand but not quite so fierce and venomous, plateau greens perched defiantly on high where the wind does indeed "play the tyrant" with the ball, greens nestling in dells, long narrow valleys and wide open stretches. It possesses, too, that natural air which is a jewel of great price. The greens though small are beautifully smooth and true, there is assuredly nothing unkempt about it, but it has not yet fallen a victim to overtreating. The fairways are not defined avenues but blend almost imperceptibly with the rough country on either side; the lies are good but the ball lies close and this ball must be hit cleanly away with a snap. The golf could be of the most tremendous championship kind by putting the tees back. When they are kept as they usually are, reasonably forward, it is the most perfect holiday golf in the world.

It is almost impossible to describe true seaside golf to those who have never had the chance of playing it. If such a one was intrusted to my care, I would take him straightway to Saunton—yes, before St. Andrews or Sandwich or anywhere—and say to him, "Now here is the real thing."